THE LINES ARE DRAWN

Other books by Gerald W. Johnson

THE LUNATIC FRINGE

OUR ENGLISH HERITAGE

THE
LINES
ARE
DRAWN

AMERICAN LIFE SINCE THE FIRST WORLD WAR
AS REFLECTED IN THE PULITZER PRIZE CARTOONS

BY GERALD W. JOHNSON

ILLUSTRATED WITH THE CARTOONS

J. B. LIPPINCOTT COMPANY
PHILADELPHIA & NEW YORK

Copyright © 1958 by Gerald W. Johnson

First Edition

Library of Congress Catalog Card Number 58-12275

Printed in the United States of America

CONTENTS

5

There were no awards in 1923, 1936.

THE LINES ARE DRAWN

INTRODUCTION

I n 1754 Benjamin Franklin published a picture in his *Pennsylvania Gazette*. It was a crude woodcut depicting a serpent divided into segments bearing the initials of the British colonies from New England to Georgia, and it bore the caption, "Join Or Die." The occasion was the outbreak of the French and Indian War, confronting the colonies with a peril that they could overcome, as Franklin believed, only by united effort.

Eleven years later a series of Parliamentary invasions of American liberty culminated in the Stamp Act. Again the colonies were confronted with a peril that they could overcome, as Franklin believed, only by united effort. Poor Richard then demonstrated his characteristic thrift; instead of having a new woodcut made, he dusted off the old one and reprinted it, with even greater effect.

This is the basis of the myth that the American newspaper cartoon originated with Benjamin Franklin and dates back to 1754. It it true only in the sense that it is true that Leif Ericson discovered America in the year 1000; that is to say, it was an event without immediate consquence. Franklin's picture was a political cartoon, and it was published in an American newspaper, but it did not establish cartooning as an element of journalism. Nearly a hundred years were to pass before that eventuated, and it came about as a result of technical advances in engraving and printing; but it had effects extending far beyond the craft of the typographers.

One of these effects was to transform the cartoonist from

an artist into a journalist—not completely, of course, but relatively. A great cartoonist is still an artist, but if it comes to that, so is a great reporter; a superb news story is as certainly literature as a superb cartoon is art. Journalism is characteristically sudden and swift; literature and art, as a rule, are slow and studied. When they become sudden and swift they take on the coloration of journalism.

It is intellectual snobbery to assume that this implies degradation, but it does imply transformation. A journalist is to be judged fairly only by the standards of his own craft, and this is true whether he writes, or speaks into a microphone, or pushes a pencil over a drawing board. If his work meets the tests of good journalism it is not to be condemned because it may not meet those of graphic art or of literature.

The history of the American political cartoon thus falls into two periods distinguished by a radical alteration in the status of the cartoonist—the period before and the period after the coming of photoengraving, the high-speed press, and other mechanical instruments of rapid reproduction. In the earlier period the cartoonist was an independent artist; in the second, beginning in the latter half of the nineteenth century, he became an organization man, charged with responsibility for only one element in a complex product that is the work of many men.

Cartooning flourished, to be sure, before this transition, but as a weapon of independent propaganda, not as a part of journalism. The cartoonist of the early days offered his work, not to newspapers, but to commercial printers, to be published in the form of a broadside and distributed through dealers in prints. Seventy years after Franklin's death the celebrated lithographers, Currier and Ives, were still handling political cartoons in this way.

But the printer, viewing the cartoon as merchandise, was cheerfully indifferent to the subject of the drawing. He wanted an article that would sell, and if the drawing had a punch it would sell, irrespective of where the punch landed. The printing houses regularly published cartoons on both sides of the same controversy, and never gave that aspect of the matter a second thought.

This complete freedom from any consideration of policy affected the cartoonist of the early days in ways that made him distinctly different from his successor, the newspaper cartoonist of today. The conditions of the earlier cartoonist's work were favorable to the development of power, but not of prudence. The result was frequently a cartoon of immense strength, but of a savagery before which our generation stands aghast.

The early cartoonist could take his own time and choose, within limits, his own medium of reproduction. This permitted delicacy and subtlety of treatment. On the other hand, the cartoon had to sell itself, lacking the support of a newspaper's circulation department, and this made against delicacy and subtlety. The newspaper cartoonist's work supports, and is supported by, the reading matter in the adjoining columns, but the broadside had to carry the whole story. For that reason the early cartoonist often felt compelled to crowd his picture with lettering, to its damage as a picture.

In other words, the primary object of the early cartoon was to create a mood by its own unaided force; the primary object of the newspaper cartoon is to establish an opinion in which it is aided by other forces, above all, that of timeliness, the seizure of the fleeting moment. This shift in emphasis is more than a shift away from the fine arts in the direction of the crafts. It is also a shift in the workman's mental attitude toward his work, and this difference must be taken into account in any fair appraisal. The modern cartoonist is not primarily an artist, but a journalist, and it is by the canons of journalism that he must be judged first.

To call Benjamin Franklin the first newspaper cartoonist is manifestly as absurd as it would be to call him the first aviator because he applied the principles of aerodynamics to flying a kite. The newspaper cartoonist, like the aviator, could not come into being until technology had advanced further than it was in Franklin's day.

But with the development of mechanical reproduction processes that were cheap and rapid the cartoon became more and more easily available to the periodical press. If any individual is entitled to be called the father of the American cartoon, a better claim than Franklin's can be made out for an odd character, originally named Henry Carter, who came to this country from England in 1848. He was by trade an engraver, but he was a man of immense ingenuity, immense energy, and a daring that surpassed both. He was by no means the first journalist to realize the news value of pictures but he was the first to do anything effective about it. A practical engraver himself, he devised and taught his employees methods of reproduction faster than any known before his time; and they gave him a dominant position in illustrated journalism.

In 1855 he set up *Frank Leslie's Illustrated Newspaper* and in five years had made such a smashing success that imitators sprang up on every hand. (In 1857 he had the courts change his name to Frank Leslie.) His interest was primarily in news pictures, but his improved processes made the timely cartoon available to the periodical press; and his place in the history of cartooning is made secure by the fact that he discovered and employed the genius of Thomas Nast, Joseph Keppler and Bernhard Gillam, among others.

Yet the American cartoon as an art form reached its highest level under other auspices, especially *Harper's Weekly,* chief rival of *Leslie's,* the original *Vanity Fair* and, somewhat later, the humorous weeklies, *Puck* and *Judge.* All these were printed on smooth stock, allowing a delicacy and precision of detail impossible on newsprint. All were strong on caricature in the European style—Gillam was an Englishman, Keppler and Nast, Germans—and *Puck* and *Judge* eventually went in for lithography in color. Finally, none appeared oftener than once a week. The result was a period when the cartoon attained high esthetic merit without much loss in either vigor or venom.

Keppler, Gillam and Zimmerman had time to spend on loving detail that could be brought out on calendered paper; they could take caricature to a high degree of subtlety; and they had a sophisticated audience, giving them an enormous advantage in the use of allusion. One of the most powerful, and surely one of the wickedest cartoons in American history was based on Gillam's assurance that most of his audience would understand an allusion to J. L. Gérôme's scandal-evoking picture, "Phryne Before Her Judges," which had been the sensation of Paris a dozen years earlier. Gillam showed Blaine being unveiled before the Republican leaders by Whitelaw Reid, revealing him hideously tattooed with the record of dubious deals; a satire on the story of the Greek orator Hypereides who won a verdict for the courtesan Phryne simply by exposing her beauty to the Areopagus. Perhaps mood, rather than opinion, was still the aim of these men; but they were edging over.

There is, therefore, reason in the assertion that what we know as the newspaper cartoon originated, not with Franklin in 1754, but with Thomas Nast, whose most memorable work was done for *Harper's Weekly* between 1862 and 1886. Even Nast, producing one cartoon a week, could spend on each drawing from three to seven times as much time as is allowed the contemporary cartoonist; and his work was printed on paper smoother than newsprint, which allowed him certain differences in style. But he did follow closely a journalistic policy in whose making others had participated. This was conspicuously true in the war against the Tweed Ring, best remembered of all Nast's adventures. His support of a journalistic policy made him essentially a journalist. His skill, indeed, made him an artist and a fine one, but it was his secondary, not his primary status.

Here, then, is the dividing line, the watershed, the Height of Land, between the old dispensation and the new. From Nast's time on, the cartoonist has been in increasing measure a journalist. Which is to say, if you choose to be stuffy about it, the Artist becomes the Artisan—although as a social force the Artisan has been worth the Artist ten times over. From the latter days of the nineteenth century the cartoonist has been restricted by consideration of policy as well as by physical conditions.

Certain physical conditions restrict his freedom, but as much is true of any pictorial representation. Even Michelangelo had to take into account the curve of the Sistine Chapel ceiling. The comparatively rough surface of newsprint requires a bold, decisive line, and the limited space allotted to the cartoon forbids the use of elaborate detail. Delicacy is not impossible in a broad, black line—witness some of the work of David Low— but great mastery of the medium is necessary to attain it. Elimination of detail ordinarily eliminates secondary themes, although some contemporary cartoonists, as Herblock, of the Washington *Post,* for instance, and Yardley, of the Baltimore *Sun,* frequently redouble the original impact of the cartoon by inserting some sly detail that registers only at the second look. But even they cannot be sure of getting that second look; they must rely on the frontal assault.

However, it is not his physical working conditions that make the cartoonist primarily a journalist and only secondarily an artist. The illustrator and the architect's draftsman also must meet a deadline, also are restricted in their choice of media, and also must be single-minded; if they are supreme masters of their crafts they may also be artists, but never journalists.

For the essence of journalism is speed of communication. Elaborate researches by many pundits indicate that the American who gives as much as an hour a day to the newspaper is exceptional; from a third to a half as long is nearer the average. This is the inescapable condition that dictates the form of the newspaper story—the fictional form in reverse, with the climax in the leading paragraph, the development following. The same necessity dictates that the cartoon shall produce its main effect in the first ten seconds of observation, for ordinarily it will not be given an eleventh second.

Obviously, then, to judge a cartoon by the criteria that one applies to an etching or a painting is nonsensical. The trite is instantly comprehensible and so meets the first qualification of a cartoon. Stupid men and lazy men never proceed beyond the first qualification, which accounts for the monstrous quantity of bad cartooning that afflicts the country. In fairness it should be added that the same weakness accounts for the monstrous quantity of bad writing that afflicts journalism.

The criteria fairly applicable to a modern newspaper cartoon include, first, a clarity that makes it instantly comprehensible. Without this it is neither good nor bad, it simply isn't a cartoon at all. It may be junk, or it may be as great a masterpiece as Meryon's "Stryge," that marvelous etching of a gargoyle on the cathedral of Notre Dame de Paris, but it isn't a cartoon. If, in addition to being clear, the cartoonist can draw, his work will be a good cartoon. If in addition to being clear and skillful he is also a wit, then his will be a powerful cartoon. If to clarity, skill, and wit, he can add understanding, then he will produce a great cartoon.

Surely, it is needless to emphasize that the great cartoon is as rare as the great portrait, or the great landscape—for that matter, as rare as the great novel or the great play—and for the same reason. It is given to few men, and to those few only after long intervals, to understand completely the situation with which they deal. In the case of the cartoonist the difficulty is increased by the fact that his situation is of the moment. If he is highly competent, his idea is drawn from the latest edition of the newspapers, possibly from a flash over the radio, which is to say, the situation is always new, frequently astonishing, and usually obscure. A man who can comprehend fully and in an instant a situation that is new, astonishing and obscure is a man inspired; and inspiration is no more common in cartooning than in any other line of human endeavor.

It is a curious fact that some men of very high general intelligence have never clearly understood this. For instance, David Low, certainly one of the ablest cartoonists alive, in his autobiography published in 1957, snaps at people who praise one of his cartoons because it contains a brilliant idea. But the idea *is* the cartoon. All else—the drawing, the caricature, the wit and, it may be, the malice—are so many means to the end, which is to say the presentation of the idea, the cartoonist's conception of the truth. What really enrages Low is the prevalent human tendency to confuse the wisecrack—or, to put it more decorously, the *jeu d'esprit*—with the idea. The flash of wit is designed, of course, to illuminate the truth, and it is, one must admit, maddening to have people perceive the flash, but miss the truth. Nevertheless, Low fell into gross error when he denied the dependence of the cartoon upon the idea.

Really great journalism, whether in the form of news reporting, of editorial comment, or of cartooning, is not the transmission of factual information, but the presentation of the truth, which often lies behind and is more or less concealed by the facts. But greatness is the gift of God, not to be commanded; so the journalist is absolved of responsibility if he sticks to the facts. This applies to the cartoonist as to the other craftsmen; yet because he works with line, not with language, he escapes the bondage of words and thus has a more direct approach to truth than either the reporter or the editorial writer. By the same token, swiftness of perception is more important to him than to any other journalist.

When Low, in 1938, drew a picture of an umbrella that was

unmistakably Neville Chamberlain, or of a Neville Chamberlain who was indubitably the umbrella that had become his totem, Low was intent upon caricature. But the success of that terrific cartoon rests, not upon the caricature of one man, but upon the idea that led to the caricature. That idea presented a truth that went far beyond Chamberlain; it was a satire that explained a nation.

In 1938 Great Britian—and for that matter all the western democracies—had become self-hypnotized to such an extent that she had lost touch with reality and had developed a fatal trust in the efficacy of the gesture. Hitler had been Chancellor of Germany for five years, but still Great Britain could not believe in the reality of what he represented, and trusted to gestures to quell him. She was like a forgotten American of nearly a century ago.

On April 19, 1861, the Sixth Massachusetts Infantry, proceeding to Washington, detrained and undertook to march through the streets of Baltimore. Stones were thrown, and the troops opened fire on the mob; eleven soldiers and thirty-five or forty civilians were killed. In this subsequent account of the rioting the hapless Mayor of the city wrote, with evident astonishment, "They did not stop, although I waved my umbrella at them."

The truth of 1938, of Berchtesgaden and Munich, is that Hitler would not stop, although Britannia waved her umbrella, *videlicet* Neville Chamberlain, at him; and Britannia was astonished. This truth David Low perceived at the time; and that perception, not its crucifixion of the luckless Chamberlain, is the greatness of his cartoon. Then when people laughed and praised him for making Chamberlain look like an umbrella, or an umbrella look like Chamberlain, as doubtless some did, it is no wonder that he was irritated.

All of which is an endeavor to explain why it is appropriate that a school of journalism rather than a school of art, should be the American Fountain of Honor, the rightful agency to confer the accolade on a cartoonist. It is because he is a journalist and when his achievement is distinguished, it is distinguished journalism.

There are, however, many schools of journalism in the

country, some of which rival the one at Columbia University in their professional competence; yet this one alone undertakes to single out, and celebrate, craftsmanship of exceptionally high quality.

It is not an educational function; it is an extra-curricular duty, and an onerous one, saddled upon it by the donor of its original endowment. This was Joseph Pulitzer, a Hungarian immigrant who landed in this country at the age of seventeen, found his way to St. Louis, got a newspaper job with Carl Schurz, combined the *Post* and the *Dispatch*, made a fortune with the merger, moved to New York and bought the *World*, multiplied his fortune, gained an immense reputation and immense power, and gave two and a half millions to Columbia University to found a school of journalism. In his will— one suspects as a sort of afterthought, rather than as one of his really ambitious projects—he left the school an additional endowment the income of which was to provide awards for distinguished achievement in journalism, literature and education.

Such was the origin of the Pulitzer Prizes, the first of which were awarded in 1917 and the first for cartooning in 1922. Their subsequent history in relation to their founder offers an instructive, if sardonic, commentary on the freakishness of human fortune.

Joseph Pulitzer, alive, was a terrific force, a many-faceted genius. He reached the United States in 1864, enlisted in the Union Army and served to the end of the war, studied law, entered politics, served in the Missouri legislature and later in Congress from New York, invented, exploited, and abandoned "yellow journalism," helped precipitate the war with Spain, got himself sued for libel by the then President of the United States, none other than the terrific Theodore Roosevelt, (the case was eventually dropped, so the facts were never established in court), and for the twenty-eight years that he controlled the *World*, ranked as one of the great lords of American journalism and one of the most powerful men in the United States.

But it is proverbial in the craft that no necropolis contains anything deader than a dead editor. As a rule his fame is more evanescent even than that of an actor. In their day Blair and Bowles were vastly more potent names than Beauregard and

17

Burnside, yet a thousand schoolboys can identify the generals for one who ever heard of the editors.

Pulitzer, however, survives. Not quite half a century after his death the name is familiar to many thousands who have a vague impression that Dana is the capital of Yemen, that Greeley tried to discover the North Pole, and that Bennett wrote "John Brown's Body." His excursions and alarums, his wars and conquest are forgotten, his fortune has been distributed, his newspaper has been merged with another, and even his school of journalism is today commonly regarded as merely an integer in the sum total of Columbia University. But the Pulitzer Prizes still make the headlines every year and as long as they continue to do so the nation will not forget the name.

The acerbity in this is evident, but one hesitates to say that Joseph Pulitzer would be much perturbed if he could know the outcome of all his labors. His sense of humor was wry, but real, and he had tasted bitterness—his millions could not save him from almost total blindness in his later years, and the affliction nearly drove him mad. Besides, his name does survive, and if the survival is due to one of his casual gestures, rather than to his studied effort, there is distinguished precedent for that. Edward III, of England, was a mighty king whose wars and loves and edicts jarred the world in his time: but of all his campaigns and conquests and greatness nothing survives except a jocosity—that gesture of picking up from the ballroom floor a lady's garter and on it founding an order of chivalry. Startling, disconcerting, without doubt, but *honi soit qui mal y pense.*

A better parallel with Pulitzer is that one out of many bankers who was "the best poet in Tuscany," that one of a prolific family who fathered a pope, that one of a princely line who brought his house to its apogee, but whose fame remains bright not for any of his deeds, but for a quality. He admired excellence in art, in literature, in philosophy, and studied how to reward it appropriately. So he became, not by legal enactment but by common consent of the great men of his time, The Magnificent, and by far the most illustrious of all the Medici.

As Cosimo was probably a greater man than Lorenzo, so perhaps there have been greater American journalists than Pulitzer. Dana, Greeley, Bowles, Medill, Ochs and others have their partisans who will concede precedence to no one; indeed, for sheer professional genius, his rival and enemy, Hearst, may have surpassed Pulitzer. But he is held in honor by the craft for reasons unrelated to professional competence, yet strong and more lasting than bronze. He devised a means of raising other men to honor, and in so doing lifted himself to an eminence as high above his competitors as Lorenzo is above the rest of the Medici.

So the subsequent history of this foundation has led to an unexpected, but perfectly natural outcome. Among newspaper men today it is agreed that Charles A., and Horace, and Samuel, and Adolph, were great men, very great men. But Joseph is The Magnificent.

When an award has been made under fixed conditions annually for more than a generation it is a reasonable assumption that examination of the series as a whole ought to reveal something and perhaps a great deal about the way of life of that generation. This is all the more plausible as regards the Pulitzer Prize "for a distinguished example of a cartoonist's work" on account of the method of selection.

From the start the school of journalism has declined the responsibility of making an arbitrary choice. It has relied on an advisory committee of a dozen members, including two or three university officials *ex officio,* but with a majority of outsiders drawn from the craft. They are invariably high-ranking journalists, often publishers and always men of established national reputation; and they are scattered geographically so as to give representation to all sections of the country.

About any such committee two or three things are self-evident. In the first place, it is not a jury of artists, but of journalists, hence it is not to be expected that its selections will present anything like a history of drawing in black-and-white, or reflect any particular trend in the world of art for the past generation.

On the other hand, these men are all experts in gauging public opinion, or at least one important segment of public opinion. Their success in life is based on this ability, for it is only on rare occasions that the press is the molder of public opinion. Normally the press is moulded by contemporary thought, and the journalist who cannot guess pretty accurately what and how his readers are thinking is not likely to remain long in the business. He will never rise to the top.

The thirty-five cartoons in this series should therefore be accepted, not as a history of the art, nor as a political history, but as tracing the sinuosities of upper-middle-class opinion for the period covered. They should not, however, be dismissed as negligible on that account. Except at moments of extraordinary crisis, when all rules collapse, upper-middle-class opinion is the most potent in the country, usually dominant. Understand it, and you have gone far toward understanding the history of the United States.

But not all the way. The history of the country includes a history of art and a social history, neither of which is represented in this series. To prove the first point, it is necessary only to note that the series includes no cartoon by Boardman Robinson and none by Art Young; and a history of American cartooning with no reference to those heavyweight champions would be a manifest absurdity. To prove the second point it is necessary only to note that there is no cartoon dealing with Prohibition and none dealing with Ku Kluxism—and that in the period from 1922 to 1958! Rollin Kirby won the prize three times, but never for one of his terrific assaults on Prohibition. Edmund Duffy also won it three times, but never for one of his smashing anti-Ku Klux cartoons.

An arresting characteristic of the series is the relative scarcity of effective caricature. This could be due to technical deficiency in the cartoonists. Caricature of a high order is the use of just sufficient distortion to bring out essential truth; it requires the rare combination of exquisitely balanced judgment and an extremely deft touch if it is to escape slumping into burlesque. First-rate caricature is not only a test of skill, it is also devilishly hard work, and it is conceivable that American cartoonists are simply not up to it.

But there is another explanation, less obvious, but equally plausible. It assumes a shift of upper-middle-class opinion unfavorable to the use of caricature, a shift that would certainly be reflected by the usual advisory committee in its choice of the prize-winning cartoon.

As regards public affairs, with which the cartoon usually deals, Thomas Nast's generation proceeded happily free from any doubt that guilt is personal. Nast operated on the theory that the crimes of the Tweed Ring stemmed primarily, not to say exclusively, from the conscious, freely chosen villainy of William Marcy Tweed and his associates. It followed that the impalement of Tweed upon any and every spear-point that Nast could bring to bear was not merely justified, it was a highly praiseworthy endeavor. With this the upper-middle-class was in complete agreement.

Lincoln Steffens, a pioneer Muckraker, started with this same idea, which is the basis of his book, *The Shame of the Cities*. But Steffens gradually changed his tune, and his influence played a large part in changing the climate of opinion. Steffens at length became convinced that the old-style political boss was less the creator than the creature of the rottenness that prevailed in municipal government half a century ago. Guilt, he found, was to a large extent impersonal, the resultant of forces operating upon the boss and far beyond his control.

That is unquestionably the opinion prevalent among well-informed Americans today. But once that opinion became dominant the spectacle of some luckless wretch, even one as reprehensible as a Tweed, transfixed by the lance of a brilliant satirist, looked less like a work of piety and even began to assume the hue of poor sportsmanship.

From this it was but a short step to questioning the value of crusading and it swiftly faded out of American journalism. No doubt some of the giants against which Pulitzer's *World* was constantly tilting were, in fact, windmills. Certainly windmills are no novelty among contemporary politicians. But there is a wide gap between that admission and the belief that they were all windmills, with no giants whatsoever. If they are all windmills, then there is no point in any tilting; controversy becomes a pointless and useless disturbance of the peace.

There is a great deal of evidence that upper-middle-class opinion has been approaching this point for some years. Of course the successful, even the moderately successful, have always been the great bulwark of conservatism; satisfied with the status they have attained, they tend to see in any kind of change more threat of loss than hope of gain; which generates impatience with the proponents of change.

For the past thirty-five years the American middle class has been remarkably successful. True, it received a horrible fright in 1929, a fright from which it did not fully recover for ten years, but it never was in serious danger of destruction and its losses—the number of its members who sank permanently into the proletariat—were inconsiderable. The rest of the time has been a success story that, as applied to a very large class, is without parallel. The middle class has strong reason to desire that things shall, on the whole, continue as they are going now.

It is only human to find wisdom and goodness in whatever contributes to one's own ease and convenience; hence the middle class inevitably finds wisdom and goodness in tranquility and immorality in disturbance. Controversy, except on essentially trivial matters, is disturbing; and so we arrive at a curious end —a conviction on the part of great numbers of Americans that controversy is essentially immoral. It is curious, because the nation had its origin in the conviction of its founders that controversy is the very life of the mind, so desirable that it is all but sacred. They carefully protected it against interference, even by the government itself.

However, it is doubtless inevitable that in this climate of opinion official distinction shall never be conferred on anything that is raucously controversial. You will find, therefore, that the persons charged with the duty of selecting a cartoon that meets the high approval of the American people, have, practically without exception, chosen a noncontroversial one, and rarely one that pins guilt on an individual, except such individuals as Hitler and Stalin concerning whose sinfulness there is no controversy.

Unfortunately, satire is controversial by definition, and the best cartoon is usually sharply satirical. It follows that the best cartoon is ruled out, as far as official distinction is concerned. It is risking little to assert that practically every man represented in this series has at some time drawn a better cartoon than the one for which he was awarded the prize. That is emphatically true of the three-time winners, Kirby and Duffy, and of the double winners, Shoemaker, Fitzpatrick, Darling, Harding and Block. It is probably true of the others.

When the clowns, in "A Midsummer Night's Dream," were casting a play to present before the Duke, Bottom, the weaver, wished to play every part that was mentioned, including that of the lion, which was nothing but roaring. He boasted so of his prowess at roaring that someone remarked that if he did it too well he would "fright the ladies" and get them all hanged. But Bottom met the objection with one of the most remarkable offers in the history of drama. "I grant you, friends," quoth he, "if that you should fright the ladies out of their wits, they would have no more discretion but to hang us: but I will aggravate my voice so that I will roar you as gently as any sucking dove; I will roar you an 'twere any nightingale."

From Nast to Davenport the American cartoon roared in a way unsuitable for ladylike ears to hear, and in point of fact it has never ceased. Art Young's voice was window-shattering, and Duffy and Herblock have at times roared in a way to fright the ladies. But not for that were they rewarded; it was when they took Bottom's line of the aggravated voice, and roared as gently as a sucking dove that the accolade fell upon them.

This is interesting, not as telling much about the cartoonists, but as revealing a great deal about the people before whom they perform. So an examination of this gentle roaring is well worth the time of any student of this republic.

1. On the Road to Moscow

Rollin Kirby, 1922

---

he Pulitzer Prize for a cartoon was first awarded to Rollin Kirby in 1922 for a relatively poor example of the cartoonist's work—poor, that is to say, as regards craftsmanship, but immensely successful as a reflection of public opinion on August 5, 1921, the day it appeared in the New York *World*.

The drawing portrays Death as a drummer, leading what at first glance seems to be an immense procession of men and women across a dreary landscape. The caption reads, "On the Road to Moscow." The kick in it is the fact that the long line of people is not a procession, it is a coffle, a convoy of slaves chained together.

It is a macabre piece. The background is as excellent a representation of desolation as Browning's in his poem about Childe Roland and the Dark Tower. Kirby doubtless had in mind a Russian steppe, but it is such a steppe as never was in this world, a distillation of vacuity, the quintessence of nothingness. The slaves plod from nowhere to nowhere, anonymous, amorphous. In the whole composition the only figure that has a name is Death.

Yet there is little doubt that this is a faithful reproduction of the average American's conception of Russia in 1921. In that year this nation was in a state of shock, confronted with what could not possibly happen, but had happened. A newspaper reporter, fighting simultaneously on four fronts, had whipped three generals, an admiral, and a field-marshal—Generals Kornilov, Denikin and Wrangel, Admiral Kolchak, and Field-

Marshal Pilsudski. Even a Marshal of France, Weygand, had barely been able to save Warsaw when the Russians were only fourteen miles away. Wrangel, last of the White Hopes, had been defeated and thrown out of Russia eight months before this cartoon was published.

These were undeniable facts, and it was an equally undeniable fact that the Russian commander and organizer of victory was a civilian journalist named Leon Trotzky. But it was a psychological impossibility for Amercians to believe that an untrained civilian could be a military genius surpassing even Pershing, let alone such minor celebrities as Napoleon, Caesar and Alexander the Great. Confronted with the incredible, they simply believed nothing whatever about Russia, except that Death held high carnival there.

To seize upon the one salient fact in a confused situation is the business of a good cartoonist and in this drawing Kirby proved that he knew his business. But to seize upon a fact is not necessarily to comprehend it. Kirby was revealing the truth not, as he thought, about Russia, but about the United States. The truth about Russia was the exact reverse. Ever since 1918 the Dance of Death, for the Russians, might lead toward any of the four points of the compass, but it was always the road *away* from Moscow. At one time or another the Allies—including the Americans—had held Archangel in the north, Kolchak had held Siberia to the east, Denikin and then Wrangel had held the Crimea to the south, and the Poles were to the west. On any road away from Moscow the Russian marched toward death.

But in this country, in 1921, the truth was as incomprehensible as the idea that any Russian could do what Nathanael Greene, the blacksmith, Andrew Jackson, the lawyer, Leonidas Polk, the bishop, and Nathan Bedford Forrest, the slave trader, had done in America—that is, win battles against professional officers. Yet with the truth dismissed from consideration nothing remained to explain recent events. Kirby's background, presenting nothing at all, is profoundly correct; it is the background against which most Americans saw the grisly figure that unquestionably was dancing through Russia.

Well-informed Americans, including the high command both military and political, had a clearer understanding of the real

ON THE ROAD TO MOSCOW.

situation, but they were not informing the people. It did not seem expedient to do so. We had just been through our first genuine blood-bath since 1865, and the high command had learned the important distinction between a professional army and a people in arms, namely, that while a professional army may be controlled by military discipline, a people in arms can be controlled only by force of public opinion.

The military command never, and the political command seldom has any firm faith in the reasonableness of public opinion. A Washington, a Jefferson, a Lincoln may believe in the wisdom of the people, but few smaller men; and if there was a Washington, Jefferson, or Lincoln on the scene in 1921 he has been mysteriously lost to view. Smaller men considered it self-evident that public opinion worships no deity except the Bitch-Goddess Success. It followed then—or so small men thought—that if the people were told that Trotzky was a tremendously able Chief of Operations, they would admire Trotzky; and if they admired Trotzky, they would admire Lenin; and if they admired Lenin, they would admire the Communist system; and if they admired Communism they would vote God knows what, but definitely not the straight Republican ticket. To stop that process at the beginning it was essential to give them no reason for admiring Trotzky; so they were given none.

Unfortunately, the result was the reverse of what was intended. The weak-minded, denied the true explanation of the success of the Red armies, proceeded to manufacture a mythical one. The discovery of military genius in an odd environment could have been understood, for it was nothing new to Americans; but, deprived of that unusual, but not unexampled explanation, the weak-minded attributed the success of the Reds to some mystical and perhaps supernatural merit in the Communist system; while the strong-minded were left in a daze that incapacitated them for any realistic appraisal of our policy in dealing with Russia—a daze that endured for thirteen years after this cartoon was published.

The natural result was a virulent infection of Communism among young intellectuals of the John Reed type on the one hand, and, on the other, dull acquiescence in a policy toward Russia so fabulously stupid that, in retrospect, it is almost incredible that even Warren G. Harding could have tolerated it.

Kirby, be it repeated for emphasis, drew many better cartoons during his long service with the New York *World;* but "On the Road to Moscow" deserved the Pulitzer Prize, for in it he summed up the moral and intellectual climate of 1921. It was, as he suggested, an intellectual and moral vacuum, a nullity of mind and spirit, in which dancing Death drew the people after it—not Russians only, but Americans of the sordid twenties as well, drawn to be cut down, not by machine guns, but by bootleg liquor, frenzied carnality, and insane stock-market gambling.

This was, to be sure, not an original idea. On the contrary, it was an exceedingly ancient one. But it remains as true now as it was in Solomon's day that "where there is no vision the people perish."

DIGRESSION ON THE MAN

This Rollin Kirby will be encountered again, for he was a tremendously important figure, so let this space be devoted to dry, biographical data. He was born in Galva, Illinois, September 4, 1875, and lived to the age of 76. His mother was a painter and it was doubtless her influence that sent him at nineteen to the Art Students' League, in New York, and after that to Paris, where he studied under James A. McNeill Whistler, at that time already an old man.

Kirby had talent and temperament. He was without doubt an artist when he returned to New York in 1900 and attempted to make a living by painting. Perhaps the conclusive proof that he was an artist was his reason for abandoning that life. When he finally received a commission it was for "a large, light, dining-room picture." Kirby hit the ceiling. He put his brushes away, took to illustrating, and in 1913 joined forces with Frank I. Cobb, editor of the *World,* to make that paper's editorial page the wonder that it was for the next ten years.

More about him later.

2. In Good Old USA

Jay Norwood Darling, 1924

In 1923 the advisory committee apparently threw up their
hands, for no award was made that year; but in 1924 it
went to Jay Norwood Darling, who signed his work
"J. N. Ding," and as "Ding" he won a popularity not exceeded
by any cartoonist of his generation.

This is not hard to understand, for Ding had two markedly
American characteristics—he could laugh at his idols and he
could out-weep Niobe any day of the week. A sentimental
humorist is unbeatable in the United States because he has
massed millions of sentimental humorists behind him. But he
had another characteristic that seems to be far less typically
American today than it was thirty years ago—a capacity for
biting contempt.

The prize-winning cartoon of 1924 bore the caption, "In
Good Old U.S.A." It is seventy-five per cent a typical Horatio
Alger story, but with a scorpion sting in the tail. Its four
cantos are (1) Herbert Hoover, orphaned at eight, had become a great mining engineer and an eminent economist; (2)
Frederick Peterson, son of a plasterer,* had become a famous
neurologist; (3) Warren G. Harding, once a printer's apprentice, had become President of the United States; (4) "but they
didn't get there by hanging around the corner drug store."

The final panel is the one that is stunning thirty-five years

* The Butler Library of Columbia University has permitted me to see
a letter from Darling in which he certifies that Dr. Peterson was aghast
when he found himself described as the greatest neurologist in the world.
He berated Darling for that, and also denied that his father was a plasterer.

IN, GOOD OLD U. S. A.

An orphan at eight is now one of the world's greatest mining engineers and economists, whose ambition is to eliminate the cycle of depression and unemployment

The son of a plasterer is now the world's greatest neurologist and his hobby is good health for poor children

A printer's apprentice is now the Chief Executive of the United States

But they didn't get there by hanging around the corner drug store

Reproduced by permission of Jay Norwood Darling and the *New York Herald Tribune*

after its first publication. As for the first three, the doctor, indeed, retains his stature, but the great mining engineer went on to encounter infinite woe as President of the United States, and about the former printer's apprentice who was President in 1923 the charitable prefer to maintain a kindly silence. The drugstore cowboys, however, are still with us, although under the name of juvenile delinquents.

It is Ding's attitude toward them that arrests attention, although it is fairly representative of the attitude of the respectable American a generation ago. To that frank adherent of hell, hanging, and calomel they were not "poor, mixed-up kids," and they were not juvenile deliquents. They were juvenile rattlesnakes, and Ding so pictured them.

Economic determinism had small place in his philosophy. He believed that the orphan at eight, and the plasterer's son, and the printer's apprentice succeeded because they chose to succeed. Luck played its part, no doubt, but Ding would have said that what luck did was make a great success out of what would have been a moderate success anyhow. It was his opinion that in nine cases out of ten diligence and determination would make an American boy a reputable member of society—not necessarily a great man, but a least a full-grown man.

For the tenth case, the diligent and resolute man pursued, as some men seem to be, by malignant fate, he had infinite charity. But his sympathy was not all-embracing. He believed in the existence of a small minority who, with full capacity for making the right choice, deliberately make the wrong one; and toward these he, like William Lloyd Garrison, was "as harsh as truth and as uncompromising as justice."

So he made the final panel of this cartoon an astounding depiction of unmodified and unmitigated worthlessness. Toulouse-Lautrec is generally accounted pretty good at portrayals of the dregs of society, but his specimens of human garbage have at least one positive quality—they have suffered, and therefore arouse some traces of pity and terror. But Ding's corner loafers have not suffered; they are as yet not even vicious, they are only vacuous. They are not potent enough to arouse his wrath, much less his fear; they stir no emotion except contempt.

In 1958 this attitude is definitely unconventional and there are those who will call it not merely unconventional, but un-civilized, or at least as archaic as the *code duello*. They hold that the modern juvenile delinquent is to be viewed with no emotion other than scientific curiosity; if he does indeed arouse both anger and fear, that is an unfortunate proof of human fallibility, and the angry and fearful should be dealt with firmly, if leniently. They should in no circumstances be allowed to deal with the delinquents.

As for contempt, however, that is utterly beyond the pale, and the contemptuous man must be put down rigorously, if necessary by force and arms. Contempt implies gradations in humanity and gradations are not permissible under the level-ing theory that seems more and more to be assuming the image and superscription of democracy.

There is, in fact, no denying that hearty contempt implies a degree of moral certitude that is inseparable from arrogance. If a man is contemptuous of the morals and manners of a ba-boon there can be no doubt that the man is immutably con-vinced of his mental and moral superiority to the baboon. There is no justification for this except the simple fact that it is true, not, perhaps, in the eyes of God, but certainly in the eyes of men.

By the same token, when a man who has worked hard and long to attain and maintain a reputable status in society, ex-hibits contempt for one who will not work at all, there can be no doubt that the worker ascribes merit to himself for his in-dustry and perseverance. Thirty-five years ago, when Ding drew his cartoon, this was generally accepted as right and proper. Industry and perseverance were then regarded not merely as virtues, but as major virtues, highly commendable.

Inevitably their opposites, sloth and irresponsibility, were branded as vices, and vice was not accepted as primarily a mis-fortune attributable to environmental influences. Ding, for example, was firmly convinced that the influence of an un-favorable environment can be overcome by diligence and good sense, and he cited the engineer, the doctor, and the President as evidence in support of his theory. The advisory committee agreed with him so thoroughly that they chose his demon-stration as the distinguished cartoon of the year.

Perhaps a graphic demonstration of equal force might be

33

chosen again, but one wonders. The ideal of equality before
the law, written into the Declaration of Independence and
buttressed by the Constitution was intended by such men as
Jefferson and Madison to be taken as written—"equality before the law." It evidently never crossed their minds that rational men would even begin to read it, equality, period. If
they failed to spell this out, it was because they assumed that
all men agreed that there are gradations, even among ideals,
and that excellence is to be preferred over equality. Jefferson
was shocked when John Adams seemed to doubt the Virginian's
belief in "a natural aristocracy among men" based on "virtue
and talents," and he hastened to profess explicity his belief in
what he had assumed to be a self-evident truth.

The plain, however deplorable, fact is that the Founding
Fathers were pretty contemptuous men. They believed that
the difference between a scoundrel and an honest man is real.
They believed that it is often, if not always and altogether, a
matter of choice. They believed that the difference is plainly
discernible in their conduct. And they believed that an honest
man's duty toward a scoundrel is to kick him. The cartoon
strongly suggests that this opinion prevailed as far down as the
year 1924, when Ding's expression of it was approved.

We are further advanced in 1958; but in which direction
we have advanced is still open to a shade of doubt.

Digression on the Man

Later there will be occasion to refer again to Jay Norwood
Darling also, so let it be mentioned here merely that he was
born at Norwood, Michigan, October 21, 1876, the son of a
Congregational minister, was educated at Beloit College in
Wisconsin, and spent most of his active life in Des Moines,
Iowa.

Ding was self-taught. He went into journalism as a reporter,
but he had long since discovered his talent for drawing. At
college while he was art editor of the student annual he made
a caricature of the faculty so effective that it got his fraternity
suspended for a year.

The popularity of his cartoons in the Des Moines *Register*

became so great that he was bombarded with flattering offers from New York and he did work briefly for the *Globe*. But nothing could divorce him permanently from Des Moines, and eventually the New York *Herald-Tribune* made the unheard-of concession of running his cartoons while permitting him to reside in Iowa.

Ding apparently knew what was good for him, physically at least, for he survived to the age of eighty, a prosperous and honored citizen of his home town, and an amazement to the New Yorkers, who could never comprehend a preference for Des Moines.

3. News from the Outside World

Rollin Kirby, 1925

I n 1925 it was Kirby again, but Kirby in a somewhat different mood. This is a laughing cartoon—with plenty of acid in the laughter, but nevertheless a jocund production.

A picture, it is said, needs no translation, but that is not quite true. This cartoon is so thoroughly American that it might puzzle a European or an Asiatic. An Australian, perhaps, might get its full force at a glance, but no inhabitant of a crowded country would be likely to appreciate the scene; it is a hobo "jungle" with three bums warming a bucket of stew over a camp fire and getting "News From the Outside World" by studying a newspaper announcing the conclusion of a peace pact among members of the League of Nations.

The jungle and the reading are the features peculiar to this country. Every nation in the world has its equivalent of the hoboes, but the existence of a jungle is incompatible with a dense population, and in most of the world a fire in the open is forbidden except in Gypsy encampments and official recreation areas. It is also a fairly safe assertion that the American 'bo is a more avid reader of newspapers than his prototype anywhere else on earth; but while others may require some explanation, any American will recognize the setting at a glance.

What may puzzle the younger generation in 1958 is the fact that the three outcasts represent Russia, Mexico and the United States. The conjunction of Mexico and this country seems natural enough today, for their interests have been bound

NEWS FROM THE OUTSIDE WORLD.

together ever more firmly during the thirty-four years since this cartoon was drawn. But Russia?

More than that, the figure of Russia looks odd, very odd in 1958. There is no suggestion of Khrushchev, or Stalin, or even Lenin in it. This is more like Count Leo Tolstoi—at his shaggiest, in the moujik dress he affected, but still the kindly old mystic, not any of the monstrous apparitions of later years. It is a Russia foreign to the experience of the younger generation.

The revelation of the drawing is that in 1925, the year the award was made, a great many people including, obviously, the Pulitzer Prize judges, regarded the absence from the League of Nations of Mexico, Russia and the United States as a great deal less than a triumph for those nations. It seemed more like an exclusion from civilized society. Perhaps it was.

It must be remembered—perhaps one should say it must be believed, for believing it is the difficult thing—that although Nikolai Lenin had died in January, 1924, in October of that year not one American in ten thousand had heard the name of Joseph Stalin. It was not until 1926, the year after this award, that Stalin emerged victorious from the struggle within the Kremlin. It was a combat of extreme ferocity, with the issue long in doubt; but the United States knew almost nothing about it, and if it had known, its withdrawal from European contacts had left it in no position to influence the outcome.

Rollin Kirby was a well-informed man, far better informed than most of his countrymen, but the relative placidity of his picture of Russia is eloquent of his ignorance of the convulsions that even then were beginning to rack Moscow. If Kirby did not know, what folly it would be to blame the mass of the voters for their total ignorance!

But the people did know, or a great many of them did, that the attempt to withdraw from the world was futile and some of them felt that it was disreputable. We tend to forget that. Many of us assume that it is historical fact that the American people practically unanimously repudiated Woodrow Wilson and his League; but in reality it took a long and desperate fight, conducted by the most skillful politicians in the country, to defeat the League. Jim Watson, an Old Guard Senator from Indiana and a bitter opponent of Wilson, once said that a popular vote taken immediately after Wilson's return from Paris would have been eighty per cent favorable to joining the League of Nations, and Jim was certainly no wool-gathering idealist. He took unabashed pride in having helped defeat what four fifths of the people believed to be right.

That is why Kirby's cartoon depicting Uncle Sam as a hobo, cut off from respectable people and knowing what they were doing only by reading about it, was singled out for distinction in 1925. The cult of the completely sovereign state was at a low ebb. Its most spectacular demonstration up to that time, the Hohenzollern empire, had come to a dramatically evil end, and although a more lurid demonstration was in the making it had not yet attracted much attention. Mussolini had marched on Rome in 1922, but in 1924 he was still a curiosity rather than the exponent of a new kind of statecraft. As for Adolf Hitler, he had just emerged from the Munich jail, and none dreamed that he was destined to stage a demonstration of statism that for garishness was to all others as the mouth of hell is to a tallow candle. He would come to an even more dramatically evil end, but not before he had infected the rest of the world with much of his frenzy.

With the inestimable advantage of hindsight we can appreciate as nobody could in 1924 the irony of the headline in the paper that Uncle Sam is reading. It runs, "Forty-eight Nations Agree Upon League Peace Pact." They agreed upon peace— with the United States and Russia left out!

It was an exhibition of futility, without doubt, but that it was an exhibition of fatuity is not so certain. Men must judge the world by what is before their eyes, and if their eyes deceive them they are not always blameworthy. In 1924 men were gazing at two shells, very formidable in appearance and as yet giving little outward indication of their hollowness. They were the French and British empires, impressive then to a degree that the modern generation finds it hard to comprehend. In 1924 few Americans doubted that the French Army was the best in the world, or that the British Navy was capable of keeping the Orient in order.

So we face the disconcerting fact that the one element in the picture that Kirby thought perfectly serious, the headline, is in truth the sharpest barb of satire in the whole composition.

The caption is hardly less so. The news was from the outside world, all right, but that world was outside in a sense that the cartoonist did not intend. The inside world comprised the denizens of the jungle; the future was in possession of the hoboes, not of the respectable citizens busily intent on establishing world order without the assistance of the only people who could preserve order.

It is plain enough now that as long as there is no real peace between the United States and Russia there will be no real peace in the world, and no better substitute than an uneasy truce with both sides armed to the teeth and constantly increasing their armaments. The thunderous end of that kind of thing, if it is kept up long enough, is a foregone conclusion, and it is not within our power to prevent it, for while one can make war it takes not less than two to make peace.

Where is the United States to find the indispensable other party? Thirty-three years ago Kirby was not without hope for he was still capable of thinking of Russia as represented by Tolstoi, and you could make peace with Tolstoi. But in the intervening years the old mystic has faded completely out of the picture; we have to do now with practical men and as regards the establishment of lasting peace it is a wan hope to expect anything practical to be done by practical men; it takes an impractical idealist to put it over.

Kirby's concept of the Russian is not ours, and that, in 1958, proves old Father Time a more corrosive satirist than Kirby ever was. For the disappearance of Tolstoi from the picture of Russia is costing the United States vastly more than the loss of the Pacific Fleet at Pearl Harbor.

DIGRESSION ON THE MAN

Rollin Kirby, the individual, was a versatile and highly cultivated man, perhaps as alert an intelligence as is to be found in the whole galaxy of cartoonists. He drew better than he wrote, but he wrote well, on an astonishing variety of subjects. Not much in the American scene eluded his eye.

This was the second time he had won the prize with a cartoon based on foreign relations, but he had won his national reputation with very different stuff. At the moment when this award was made preparations were under way for the fantastic Scopes trial, at Dayton, Tennessee, when a young schoolteacher was haled before the bar charged with the crime of explaining to schoolboys the Darwinian theory of the origin of species, which the law of Tennessee still forbids any public schoolteacher to expound as truth; and William J. Bryan and Clarence Darrow seized the opportunity to engage in a forensic combat over the descent of man.

The stench of political corruption in Washington was becoming unbearable. An obscene burlesque of the original Ku Klux Klan was being played in Oregon and Indiana, as well as along the Gulf coast. The orgy of crime attendant on Prohibition was gathering momentum.

The keen of eye of Kirby missed none of these things, and his best work was done in defending common decency against them. But that work was controversial and prudent awarders of prizes may have come and looked on such, but they passed by on the other side.

4. The Laws of Moses and the Laws of Today

D. R. Fitzpatrick, 1926

Georges Clemenceau, confronted with Fourteen Points in which he did not believe but on which peace after the First World War had to be based, was restrained by diplomatic considerations from any kind of explosion except an explosion of wit; so his comment on the document was simply that whereas God Almighty was content with Ten Commandments to establish His law, Woodrow Wilson required fourteen. In this remark the Frenchman was echoing, consciously or not, the judgment of an Englishman. "A cynic devil in his blood," said Kipling of the American, is the thing

> That makes him make the law he flouts,
> That makes him flout the law he makes,

in a manner incomprehensible to the older and more settled nations of Europe.

In this cartoon, winner of the Pulitzer Prize in 1926, D. R. Fitzpatrick, of the St. Louis *Post-Dispatch,* apparently had in mind Clemenceau's sarcasm, for he shows the Mosaic tablets overshadowed by "the laws of today." But he seems to have found no trace of Kipling's cynic devil; on the contrary, he represents the American as a pathetic figure with gyves on his wrists and dragging a ball and chain.

THE LAWS OF MOSES AND THE LAWS OF TODAY.

Although it was published April 12, 1925, a whole generation ago, this is one cartoon of which it is safe to say that it has remained timely for thirty-three years. The American still has, as he had in 1925, and has always had, a curiously ambivalent attitude toward the law, respecting it in principle while blithely disregarding it in practice. Foreigners take it as an attitude of basic contempt, but it may be plausibly argued that it is one of too much respect for law.

A few years before 1925 some ingenious contriver of gadgets had cleaned up a fortune by manufacturing a squat caricature of a Buddha and selling it for a mascot under the title, "Billiken, God of Things as They Ought To Be." In a somewhat obscure fashion the American has always paid his devotions to law as a sort of god of things not as they are, but as they ought to be. The law must be perfect; and if in attaining perfection in an imperfect world, it acquires an incongruity that often gives it a touch of the comic, the American is no more disturbed by that than he is by the fatuous grin on the face of Billiken.

In 1925 the United States was just beginning to feel the effects of a particularly unfortunate example of this addiction to Billiken-law. It was universally agreed that men ought to be temperate in all things, specifically in the use of alcoholic beverages. Hence it was argued that if the law represents things as they ought to be, the law should enforce temperance. Unfortunately, the definition of temperance was left to the intemperate, that is, to fanatics who construed it as total abstinence —as far from moderation, on the one side, as drunkenness is on the other.

The result, of course, was not to abolish liquor, but only to make most liquor indescribably bad. The potable kind was made so frightfully expensive that only the rich could afford it; but raw spirits, wretchedly distilled and unfit for human consumption, being relieved of all taxation, became cheaper than before adoption of the Prohibition Amendment. As the first simple enactments failed, more and more laws were passed until in some states the output became fantastic; and as more and more grotesquely excessive punishments were prescribed, juries became more and more reluctant to convict, no matter how strong the evidence. Yet it took fourteen years to bring the country to admit that the law had defeated itself.

This is without doubt part of what Fitzpatrick had in mind when he drew this cartoon but it was not all, by any means. A hundred social problems other than that of alcoholism have produced thousands of statutes based on the theory that the law is not the summation of sensible men's opinion of what can be done, but the expression of an ideal, whether attainable or not.

When the ideal is not attainable, the law expressing it becomes a dead letter. One of the most pernicious fallicies current in American political philosophy is the delusion that this does not matter. Otherwise intelligent people permit themselves to think that when a law becomes a dead letter it falls into what Grover Cleveland—perhaps with his tongue in his cheek—called "innocuous desuetude." Desuetude means simply disuse, but in the case of a law it is rarely, if ever, innocuous because at any time it may become very noxious indeed. Cleveland, as a matter of fact, was citing an instance of that very thing when he coined the phrase. He was protesting against revivals of the Tenure of Office acts, originally passed to handicap Andrew Johnson, but: "After an existence of almost twenty years of nearly innocuous desuetude these laws are brought forth" to hamstring President Cleveland!

A dead-letter law may be of no other use, but while it remains on the books it may be dragged out to prevent someone from doing what is, in new circumstances, obviously right; and sometimes it serves the vindictive as a whip with which to scourge persons whom they dislike but who cannot be touched by the living law. Fitzpatrick, therefore, was truthful in decorating the citizen, bowing before the mountain of laws, with fetters and a ball and chain.

As in every good cartoon, the keynote that this one strikes is attended by innumerable harmonics, overtones that in this instance do not originate in legislative halls. The lawmakers are not spurred to such prodigious activity solely by their own superabundant energy. The drive is supplied by their constituents, by the public pressure expressed in the constantly repeated assertion, "There ought to be a law."

Nine times out of ten this is the reverse of the truth. Nine times out of ten there ought not to be a law. The condition complained of—if it needs remedying, which is not always the case—ought to be corrected by public opinion resulting in private initiative, not by statute. The law can deal with crime, but not with sin. The law is a scatter-gun, not a rifle, and to use it against a hawk in the chicken-yard means that while you may get the criminal or may not, you are practically certain to knock over a dozen fat hens with the same blast.

Robert Burton, great predecessor of the psychiatrists, observed that he who invokes the law has a wolf by the ears, which he called a proverb old even in his time; but the American people have not learned it yet, although Burton has been dead more than three hundred years. As regards private lawsuits we know it; every good lawyer tries to keep his client out of court. But as regards the making of laws we cannot realize that every new statute is a new link in our chains. Some of these links are necessary evils to prevent worse evils, but all are evils. As they proliferate, so inevitably does crime, and the chain gang lengthens with the code.

Digression on the Man

Daniel Robert Fitzpatrick (who will appear again in this list) was born in Superior, Wisconsin, in 1891, and has claimed that he was kicked out of high school at the age of sixteen for "wasting his time" in drawing when his attention was supposed to be centered on algebra and history.

At any rate, he went to the Chicago Art Institute for a couple of years and after that worked briefly for the *Daily News* in that city. But he found his real place in the scheme of things when he took service with Joseph Pulitzer's original newspaper, the *Post-Dispatch,* of St. Louis.

Man and organization fit like hand and glove for, although it is part of Fitzpatrick's arrangement with the paper that he will never be called on to draw a cartoon taking a position with which he does not agree, the policy of the newspaper has been in general parallel with Fitzpatrick's conviction.

As a result he obtained a position in the estimation of Mississippi Valley newspaper readers that few cartoonists have attained—not quite oracle and not quite Peck's Bad Boy, but a sort of combination of both, admired and denounced, both extravagantly, but almost always consulted before readers made up their minds.

That is to say, Fitzpatrick has been important for more years than some very clever cartoonists have lived.

5. Toppling the Idol

Nelson Harding, 1927

The cartoon with which Nelson Harding won the prize in 1927 would not stand a chance thirty years later. Indeed, such a paper as the Brooklyn *Eagle* was then—today, alas, the *Eagle* is one with Nineveh and Tyre —would not publish the cartoon, not because our standards of drawing have risen, but because our hopes have sunk.

Harding depicted a group representing the League of Nations in the act of dragging the statue of Mars off its pedestal. It didn't happen, and we no longer expect it to happen. Indeed, we no longer want it to happen, for things are now at such a pass that if the statue were toppled the economic system of the United States certainly, and perhaps that of the whole world, would be crushed by its fall.

The cartoon was published September 19, 1926. By that date in 1956 we had worked ourselves into such a snarl that war *in posse,* although not *in esse,* had become essential to the functioning of the national economy. That is to say, a sudden cessation of the expenditure of ten per cent of the national income on armament, or for some equally nonproductive purpose, would have had disastrous effects—terrific unemployment, bankruptcy of the steel industry and many of its collaterals, such as aircraft and automobiles, ruin of petroleum, and appalling agricultural surpluses.

Our system of distribution was geared to handle only about ninety per cent of our total production through peacetime channels. The remaining ten per cent was enough to choke the normal arteries of trade, producing an economic throm-

TOPPLING THE IDOL

Reproduced by permission of Nelson Harding and the *Brooklyn Daily Eagle*

bosis of incalculable but frightening extent. The process of distribution had to be stepped up by some means not envisaged in the economics of Adam Smith. We found it by withdrawing three million men from the labor force and ten per cent from income, and devoting both to defense.

To be sure, the ingenious Scot had long since been deposed as the high priest of the Faculty of Economics, but millions of laymen did not know it. They still had implicit faith in the canon law as laid down in *The Wealth of Nations,* and any departure from it could be justified, in their opinion, only to meet some threat to the existence of the nation, presumably war or the threat of war requiring enormous defensive armament.

Fortunately for our political leaders, the Russians accommodated them by supplying the necessary threat. By every standard of judgment they did mean mischief, and the necessity of arming was real enough. But if the Russians had not existed we should have had to devise some other means of getting rid of thirty to forty billions a year in order to keep the economic system operating smoothly; and to spend that much money for any nonproductive purpose except arms might have precipitated a revolution, so thoroughly were our people imbued with the philosophy of Adam Smith. Even today, the suggestion that the embarrassing ten per cent might well be spent on cultural, not economic, values—schools, parks, playgrounds, public recreation—is darkly regarded as socialistic if not communistic. The fact that one of its real recommendations is that it seems to be essential to the preservation of capitalism is blandly ignored.

So Harding's cartoon of 1926 is literally something out of another world. It was a world in which cartoonists portrayed war as the abysmal brute, yet definitely a brute, a sentient creature, in fact an anthropoid, just below the level of the human. Some years were to pass before it was gradually divested of every attribute of the primates and was resolved into a mechanism, the interplay of blind forces before which both man and brute are helpless.

Harding's Mars was closer to a gorilla than to a man, but at that it was a relatively hopeful portrayal. After all, man had subdued the apes, including the most powerful among them;

so if war were basically no more than a somewhat larger ape, there was reason to believe that it, too, might eventually be subdued.

That was, without doubt, the belief of most intelligent men a little more than thirty years ago, and the cartoonists reflected it accurately. Compare it with the conventional modern representation. Occasionally the Greek hoplite or the Roman legionnaire is used; but more often war is a tank, a car of Juggernaut, or, recently, interlaced elipses with a central dot, the symbol of the atom. And that, too, reflects the thinking of its day. "Toppling the Idol," Harding's subject, is a relatively simple operation, requiring only a stout hawser and a strong pull; but dismantling a machine is far more complex, and very much more complex is the job if proving that some incomprehensible mathematical formula is not a recipe for happiness, but a *reductio ad absurdum*.

Nevertheless, such is the task facing members of the contemporary generation who don't want to be vaporized. "Patriotism is not enough," cried Nurse Cavell; but today she should add, "nor is pacifism enough."

To get rid of war is certainly the prime necessity of the modern world, since war has become as destructive to the victors as to the vanquished, and perhaps more ruinous to neutrals than to either. But after that, what? The dozen years following the "cease fire" of 1945 convinced vast numbers that absence of active hostilities could be more nerve-racking than war. While the fighting continued we took it for granted that the enemy was making every possible effort to obtain military information—not merely "military intelligence," that is, information about the armed forces, but any and every kind of knowledge that might contribute to military success—yet the assumption that spies were doing their utmost did not cause us concern that amounted to an obsession.

Only after the cessation of hostilities, that is to say, after the idol of Mars was theoretically toppled, did fear of the enemy agent become so all-pervading that sober-minded students of public affairs began to envisage the possibility of our repudiating the freedom we had fought to defend replacing it with a police state.

Nor was that all. Thirty years after Harding drew his cartoon we faced another aspect of the question that he never visualized. The national economy had been so deeply committed to high expenditures for armament that the sudden cessation of such expenditures would certainly have precipitated disaster. So it became evident that the idol cannot be toppled; if it is to be removed it must be lowered gently and carefully to avoid smashing everything built around its base. Such an operation calls for a great deal more than a hawser and plenty of manpower; it requires skillful engineering and extensive and expensive equipment. As long as there remain many who can't see the need for either, hope of the elimination of war is likely to remain dim.

It was a simpler world in 1926—or was it? In any situation hope is a factor that gives rise to complications. The simplest of all worlds is that of a man who is to be hanged tomorrow, for it is one from which hope has been eliminated. To the extent that the present-day world believes that war is inevitable and inevitably disastrous, it is a simpler world than Harding's. The theory that war may be discarded as an instrument of national policy draws in its train a host of complications, for there are a thousand ideas as to how war may be discarded.

Perhaps we should look upon the world that was impressed by this cartoon as a highly complicated world from which we have emerged into one far simpler. Of course, attainment of simplicity is not necessarily occasion for dancing in the streets. It may be the arid and grisly simplicity of Death Valley.

DIGRESSION ON THE MAN

Nelson Harding (who will appear not only again but immediately) was a product of Brooklyn and for twenty-five years an ornament of the *Eagle* thereof. He acquired his technique at the Art Students' League and the New York School of Art, where he studied under Robert Henri; but his special quality is unaccountable, as, indeed, it always is in a man of genius.

Harding was born in 1879 and lived to the age of sixty-eight in active practice as a cartoonist to within two years of his death in 1947. At nineteen he was swept into the excitement of the war with Spain and actually participated in the action at

San Juan Hill and then at Santiago—with the exception of Bill Mauldin the one actual man-at-arms in the list.

In 1929 he crossed the East River to join the staff of the New York *Journal,* with which paper he remained until his retirement in 1945.

6. May His Shadow Never Grow Less

Nelson Harding, 1928

Nelson Harding is the only cartoonist who won the Pulitzer Prize in two successive years. He was given the distinction in 1928 as he had been given it in 1927.

His second winning cartoon is an echo of one of the most romantic episodes in American history. In 1927 Charles A. Lindbergh, a professional air-mail pilot, did what no man had ever done before—he flew non-stop from New York to Paris in a single-engined plane, without radio communication and without the slightest hope of rescue in case of either mechanical or human failure. The flight was a terrific test of skill, courage and endurance, but the young American met the test with resources to spare. A prize of $25,000 had been offered for the first flight from New York to Paris and he won it, but the prize-money turned out to be a mere bagatelle, for he also won the adulation of the world in a measure rarely accorded any man.

Someone has remarked that it was a moment when a disillusioned and disgusted country greatly needed a hero, and Lindbergh met its requirements perfectly. Young, handsome, brave and modest, he had everything that a hero-worshiping public could desire. Nor did he capture the American imagination alone. Paris was delirious with enthusiasm over him, and all the other nations applauded.

Among them was our neighbor to the south. For many years Mexico had had small reason to look with approval on anything American and only a decade earlier the two countries had been

MAY HIS SHADOW NEVER GROW LESS

at open, if undeclared war; but the gallantry of the young man made a strong appeal to the Mexican people. The opportunity was seized by the astute ambassador that President Coolidge had sent to Mexico with instructions to do everything possible to establish friendlier relations. This was Dwight W. Morrow, who made millions at the law and in banking, largely through his ability to understand other men.

Morrow had already made encouraging progress with his difficult task, but he realized that for the United States to send its new hero on a good-will flight to Mexico would be a gesture that might well delight our neighbors more than all his diplomatic overtures. Washington fell in with the suggestion and the popular response in Mexico was all that could be desired.

It was this flight that Harding chose as the subject of his cartoon. It was published by the Brooklyn *Eagle* on December 15, 1927, just as the Christmas season was approaching, which inspired the cartoonist to work the religious motive into the shadow of the plane, and to inscribe the angelic chorus upon the Cross.

It was tremendously effective, yet thirty years later one can hardly avoid speculating on what a cartoon Harding might have drawn had he had a touch of the soothsayer in his blood. For while the Mexicans were pleased, Lindbergh's greatest personal triumph was not his success in pleasing them, but in pleasing the brilliant young daughter of the ambassador, Anne Morrow, who, as Anne Morrow Lindbergh, achieved a distinguished literary career and, as the wife of a popular idol, trod the steep and stony road that is reserved for American popular idols.

The story is an old, familiar one. The mob that will raise a mortal to the skies, at the first misstep will turn upon and rend him. Yet the first tragic chapter of the story was not the fault of Lindbergh nor that of the public. The murder of his child was simply an outbreak of the monstrous greed that lurks beneath the veneer of civilization in every country, and that will stop at no infamy. The fame of the Lindberghs did indeed sharpen the agony and draw it out excruciatingly, but the tragedy itself was one that might have happened to anybody. In that case they were penalized merely for being parents.

It was years later that Lindbergh paid the price for the

adulation of 1927. In part he was a victim of the wretched human propensity to drag down anyone who is elevated to a great height, but in part it was his own fault. As war was approaching with the end of the thirties, he made an unfortunate speech at Des Moines, Iowa, in which his phrasing seemed to attribute to some men inferiority on account of their race and religion. At the very moment this same attribution of inferiority in Germany was giving rise to horrors that revolted the civilized world, even though their full extent was not guessed at the time. Naturally, the mere suspicion of alignment with the enemies of the human race was not only fatal to Lindbergh's popularity, but compelled his removal from any conspicuous part in the war effort then beginning.

Harding's pious hope was defeated. The hero's shadow had grown less, almost to the vanishing point.

Yet in the years that followed the man rehabilitated himself by a remarkable demonstration of restraint, good sense and unquestionable loyalty. This deepens the mystery of why he was guilty of such egregious folly in the early days of the crisis.

In view of the subsequent record no fair-minded man can believe now that the Des Moines speech really meant what it said. It is not humanly possible that such a man as Lindbergh approved the obscenities practiced publicly and the unspeakable horrors perpetrated secretly in the name of racial superiority. It is possible, of course, that he was trapped by intellectual arrogance. It is obvious that he did not believe the reports that were coming out of Germany. Wiser men than Lindbergh have found it hard to believe that persons whom they disliked were telling the truth, and he violently disliked the men then in office in Washington.

But it may be that there was a subtler and stronger influence operating in this case. No reader of his own story, written years later, of his flight in 1927 can doubt that the man is a poet, although obviously not a poet of the conventional type. He is enchanted, not by music, but by power. It is an uncommon, but by no means an unheard-of rapture. Henry Adams, contemplating the dynamo at the Paris Exposition of 1900, was seized with a sort of nympholepsy as unmistakably poetic in essence as Coleridge's opium-induced vision of

Xanadu. The fact that you and I may be oblivious of the lyrical element in the movement of a piston rod, in the precise meshing of gears or in the exact delivery of an electrical charge is not proof that the lyricism doesn't exist, but only that you and I are not attuned to it.

But the universal poet is so rare that we can count his numbers on our fingers. Perhaps Shakespeare had no discoverable blind spot, but can that be said of any other who wrote in English? Generally speaking, we count it unfair to expect him who sings charmingly of the loves of Daphnis and Chloë to write equally well of the wrath of Peleus' son; and if they write differently, why should not the poets' sources of inspiration differ?

Lindbergh was shown in Germany an operation of power that unquestionably was among the most remarkable displays in all history, and he responded. Unfortunately, he had a blind spot that prevented him from judging the reliability of men with anything like the accuracy of his judgment of machines; so in this case he failed to estimate rightly how much of what he saw was genuine power and how much skillfully disguised showmanship. Slow to appreciate the poetry of the human drama, he failed to separate drama from melodrama. There is no reason to doubt the sincerity of his belief that the United States, in challenging Nazi Germany, was committing suicide; for he had no inkling of the truth that what his countrymen lacked was not power, but the knack of displaying it impressively.

Here, unquestionably, is an American story that in years to come will challenge the genius of some great man of letters. Contrary to Harding's hope, the shadow did grow less. But perhaps some future generation, aided by the magic of another kind of poet, will see it increase until it shall be greater than ever.

DIGRESSION ON THE MAN

Possibly the same spirit of adventure that sent him to San Juan made Harding susceptible to the daring of Lindbergh's flight, but it is more likely that his thorough-going Americanism accounts for it.

Both his prize-winning cartoons are completely serious, but for all that the man was a humorist and much of his work was in the nature of puncturing inflated pomposities. His very American dislike of posturing was evidenced when the reporters swarmed around to interview him after his winning the Pulitzer Prize twice in succession. "You may say," he told them, "that I owe my success to lots of spinach, or never going out without rubbers, or anything else that occurs to you."

He actually owed it to hard work and common sense, meaning by that an extraordinary perception of the way things would strike the average American. But how can you make a story out of that? Harding knew that you can't, so he helped the boys out with a bit of fantasia; and in that he was as American as Mark Twain and Will Rogers in their best vein.

7. Tammany

Rollin Kirby, 1929

I n 1929 Rollin Kirby was given his third award, making him the official Grand Champion American cartoonist, a title undisputed until Edmund Duffy matched the record in 1940.

Kirby's third winner is much more in line both with the bulk of his work and with the tradition of political cartooning than were his earlier successes. His "Tammany!"—note well the exclamation point—is witty, partisan, and stinging, in all of which it is traditional. The figure of the Grand Old Party upraising hands of holy horror at mention of the Democratic Tammany machine is itself a masterly portrayal of Pecksniffian hypocrisy; but the shattering impact is delivered by the angelic choir behind and above him—all prominent Republican politicians, all guilty of practices that were dubious, to put it mildly, while four were already in convicts' stripes and a fifth was soon to be.

At the time this drawing was published by the New York *World* (September 24, 1928) Albert B. Fall, formerly Secretary of the Interior, had not yet been convicted of bribe-taking, so he is not given the prison garb he was soon to wear; but he is pictured carrying the "little black bag" which was deposited on his desk with $100,000 inside after he had secretly leased the Navy's reserve oil lands to certain petroleum operators. Forbes, head of the Veterans' Bureau, Miller, Alien Property Custodian, and McCary, Governor of Indiana, went up for plain stealing—well, rather fancy stealing if one is to be precise—but D. C. Stephenson was by long odds the most fragrant flower in

the whole bouquet. He was the Republican boss of Indiana and a high official of the Ku Klux Klan. He went to the penitentiary for second-degree murder, the charge being that he drove a young woman to suicide by perpetrating unprintable atrocities upon her.

These are the characters that Kirby equipped with wings and massed behind the pompus old fraud representing the party. There is no special effort at caricature in the faces. Kirby was careful to make them instantly recognizable. The satire is in the wings and the saintly robes attached to persons such as these, and in the fact that the heavenly radiance in which the party stands is composed of dollar signs.

Thirty years later there is a corrosive irony in this that Kirby didn't put there. There was truth in the drawing and all men knew it. Nevertheless, six weeks after it was published the G.O.P. won a popular majority of six millions at the polls, and more electoral votes than any candidate except Franklin D. Roosevelt ever got; for there were not so many electoral votes in 1820 when James Monroe took all but one. The evil-smelling record proved to be no handicap at all because it was more than offset by a worse handicap upon the opposition party by race and religious prejudice.

In 1924 the Democratic party had committed the loudest and most spectacular suicide the world ever saw prior to Hitler's. Technically, at the convention in Madison Square Garden in New York William G. McAdoo and Alfred E. Smith had fought a hundred and two rounds and had knocked each other out; whereupon the nomination was given to an amiable bystander named Davis, who didn't want it and had no idea what to do with it, so he did nothing. Fatuously, some prominent Democrats mistook the technical bout in the Garden for the real war—that is to say, they thought the racial and religious issues injected into the convention had been cooked up by factional leaders for their own purposes. It was assumed that if peace could be made among the leaders these hobgoblins would vanish. So in 1928 they held a peaceable convention and gave the nomination to one of the late contestants, Smith. But instantly the hobgoblins rose again, not among the politicians, but in the electorate, and raged with such fury that they shattered the Solid South and caused the endorsement of the G.O.P., angelic choir and all.

The irony in this was the attitude of American Protestantism. The objection to Smith was (1) that he was a Catholic, and (2) that he opposed prohibition. A large segment of Protestantism, especially in the south, had long equated prohibition with religion, so both counts may be regarded as religious. At the time of the Reformation, the origin of Protestantism, one of the strongest charges that Luther brought against the Church of Rome was the practice of selling indulgences, that is to say, advance pardons for sins and even crimes committed by those who were faithful to the Church. Yet in 1928 American Protestantism sold to the Republican party indulgences for crimes ranging from theft and bribery to rape and accessory to murder —possibly first-degree murder if Jess Smith's convenient "suicide" just as he was threatening to turn State's evidence was actually assisted by minions of the Attorney General, as was suspected but never proved.

Kirby didn't get this irony into his cartoon because when he made the drawing the depth and virulence of religious prejudice had not yet been demonstrated. The demonstration came in the election six weeks later and went, if not unnoted, at least disregarded; for to this day all American politics, in both parties, seems to be wedded to the delusion that what ought to be is, or if it is not at the moment, a law will make it so. Then when it turns out that a great many things that ought not to be are, we are overcome with astonishment.

This facet of American character became conspicuous again in the years immediately after 1954. A substantial majority of Americans, a majority reaching practical unanimity in those regions where race problems are not acute, long ago became convinced that second-class citizenship is impractical and immoral in a country professing adherence to the Declaration of Independence. Then when the Supreme Court undertook to implement that conviction by outlawing racial segregation in the public schools, many well informed persons were amazed by discovering that second-class citizenship does exist and that millions of Americans defend it with immense vigor and tenacity.

Sardonic fate has decreed that again the embarrassment arising from this condition shall fall mainly upon the Democratic party, for the hard core of its voting strength is precisely among those segments of the population that believe most strongly in second-class citizenship. They demonstrated in 1928 that what the rest of the nation regards as prejudice, they regard as principle; and even corruption in government they will dismiss lightly when what they deem their racial and religious principles are involved.

It is certainly arguable that this ought not to be so, but it is so. It was so in 1928, as Kirby found out in November of that year. Thus we arrive at the curious but hardly avoidable conclusion that this very powerful cartoon was in point of fact quite irrelevant. It had no bearing on the real situation. Suppose the G.O.P. was attended by a swarm of doubtful characters and by some who were not doubtful at all, but revealed by due process of law as among the most thorough-paced villains that ever disgraced American public life—what of it? That did not alter the fact that the G.O.P. could be warranted to keep the Pope out of the White House, which a sufficient percentage of the voters thought far more important than keeping thieves out of the cash drawer.

Guessing correctly what the American voter holds sacred in any given year is the difficult but fascinating art by which a politician survives long enough to become Chairman of the Senate Finance Committee. Few there be who can master it, and if the few do not include an ingenuous newspaper cartoonist, that is no cause for wonder. Humor, reason, and technical skill are his implements and if they sometimes break in his hands, there is no remedy. Cicero said it. *Silent leges inter arma* can be construed as, when race and religion get into a campaign, all bets should be declared off.

DIGRESSION ON THE MAN

Since this is the last time we shall meet Rollin Kirby in the course of this study it is fitting to make note here of his special position not merely in cartooning but in the craft of journalism. He served and did his most brilliant work under the leadership of Frank Irving Cobb, ablest driver of spirited horses that

American journalism has yet produced, not forgetting even Harold Ross, genius of the *New Yorker*.

Cobb could handle simultaneously such divergent personalities as Kirby, Walter Lippmann, Heywood Broun, Deems Taylor and Franklin P. Adams, making each contribute in his individual style to the totality that was the New York *World*. First-rate men are strong-minded men, and a chief who can handle even two strong-minded subordinates is good; one who can handle half a dozen is masterly.

It is no deprecation of Kirby's genius to suggest that it was tempered and sharpened by collision with the hard and powerful intelligence of Cobb. If a newspaper cartoonist is a man of genuine talent in his own right, then the most valuable bit of luck that can befall him is to serve under an editor of equal intelligence and of superior determination.

Kirby, of course, would have made his mark anywhere. But it is doubtful that he would have dominated the field as absolutely as he did if he had served under any other leadership. If that is a tribute to Cobb, it is well deserved.

8. Paying for a Dead Horse

Charles R. Macauley, 1930

I n 1930 the Brooklyn *Eagle* scored again, this time with a different cartoonist, C. R. Macauley. His drawing was published in the issue of February 23, 1929, but it would have been timely on any day since and, unhappily, will probably be timely on any day for another thirty years and perhaps much longer.

It portrays a citizen of the world staggering under a tremendous burden labeled "Reparations" and leaving behind him a remarkably repulsive carcass labeled "War." The caption is one of the most dismal expressions in folklore, that melancholy phrase, "Paying for a Dead Horse."

To bring the cartoon right up to the minute only one change need even be considered, and that one is not essential. The burden might now be labeled "Defense Budget," but the rest can stand. This is because the word "reparations" acquired a special meaning after 1918. It lost part of its dictionary meaning, amends in general, and became restricted to a narrower significance, the theoretical financial penalty imposed upon defeated Germany by the victorious Allies. More than ten years after the cessation of hostilities that bookkeeper's figure was still complicating all diplomacy and clogging the channels of international trade. In the end it was extinguished by the simple process of striking it off the books, but not until another and more terrible war was in the making.

In retrospect this obsession has the look of one of the most curious episodes in modern history, even the fantastic history of the twentieth century. Granting that politicians seeking

PAYING FOR A DEAD HORSE

Reproduced by permission of Charles Macauley and the *Brooklyn Daily Eagle*

votes created the obsession by promising the people that the war would be paid for by the enemy, why should rational people have believed such an obvious lie? From the beginning wise men, and men who were not especially wise but merely rational students of economic theory, knew that the collection of reparations from a hostile nation is impossible, except for such loot as may be seized then and there and carried off by the army of occupation.

A few centuries ago it could be a profitable operation, but long before 1914 the expense of war had grown so terrific that at the end all the movable booty available would cover only a tiny fraction of the total cost. The only way to assure future collections is to maintain an army of occupation; but the expense of maintaining the army would eat up most of the collections, to say nothing of the certainty that the tensions created would lead to another war.

In view of this definite knowledge, the way in which the nations clung to the fiction of reparations year after year—the United States leading, for the so-called "war debts" were of the same nature as reparations—although the fiction was making the restoration of world trade on a stable basis impossible, seems downright insane. One looks in vain for a historical parallel, unless it is in the dancing mania of the Middle Ages, when whole populations went crazy *en masse*.

The obvious explanation, as startling as the phenomenon it explains, is that the world, if not definitely psychotic, was not quite sane. The then President of the United States, commenting on the war debts, said, "They hired the money, didn't they?" which had just about as much bearing on the question as the Biblical crackling of thorns under a pot. If Calvin Coolidge was a trifle touched in the head in those days, why expect sanity elsewhere?

The fact is that from 1914 through 1918 the western nations, including the United States, had been subjected to physical and emotional strains exceeding anything in their previous experience as far as the Black Death exceeded anything in the previous experience of those who fell to compulsive dancing in the Middle Ages. Psychologists are agreed that the horror of the plague broke the contact with reality of many thousands of medieval Europeans. The frenetic dancing was merely a symptom of that break.

The First World War had a similar effect. In soldiers extreme cases were recognized and diagnosed as "shell shock." But milder cases in the civilian population were never recognized, least of all by the victims, who were wont to view their very aberrations as conclusive proof of their sound common sense. But they were shocked out of the ability to reason. Why else did we enact the Prohibition Amendment? Why else were the illiterate enthralled by the Ku Klux Klan, and the high-and-mighty by the Smoot-Hawley tariff? Why else the stock-gambling mania that led to the crash of 1929? Why else the Mitchell Palmer witch hunt?

If we escaped some—we did not escape all—of these manifestations after the second and worse world war, two reasons for that relative immunity are plain. One is that in the second conflict war financing maintained some slight relation to reality. At the end there were neither reparations nor war debts to confuse and frustrate us. In addition to that, in the period between the wars, tales of Raw-Head and Bloody-Bones had been the staple of the day's news. Mussolini, Hitler, Stalin and Franco had inured us to the blood, butchery and the thousand forms of bestiality that accompany modern war. The shock was cushioned the second time.

But at that we are still paying for the dead horse, and shall continue to pay through the predictable future. When eighty cents out of every dollar of the government's income goes for wars, past, present, and to come, there can be no denying that we stagger under as heavy a load as the luckless wight in Macauley's cartoon.

Inevitably, then, the question arises, are we completely sane, or relatively nearer sanity than we were when this picture was drawn in 1929? It is hard to say, for the man who answers either yes or no will instantly run into embarrassing facts. Neither the Ku Klux nor the Anti-Saloon League has gained dominance this time, and the folly of anything like the Smoot-Hawley tariff is clearer to great industrialists today than it was to the professional economists in 1929. To that extent we are saner.

But to meet "a clear and present danger" two methods are

obvious. One is to increase defenses. The other is to reduce the risk. Thirteen years after the end of the great war we are still buttressing our defenses to the tune of some thirty-five billions a year; and to reduce the risk we devote some three and a half billions. The latter figure measures our effort to restore the world economy to a stable basis, since we know that a smoothly operating economy tends to eliminate the desperation of huge populations that is the fruitful mother of wars.

Apparently, then, we are laying odds of ten to one on "reeking tube and iron shard," against the promotion of human welfare as a preventive of war. This may be the height of sanity, but there are those who presume to doubt it.

Yet there is something to be said on the optimistic side. A man who realizes that his control is slipping is by no means lost to reason; the shock of the realization may restore his balance with remarkable speed. The Supreme Court decisions of 1957 were a jolting reminder of the truth of Franklin's saying that a people who will yield essential liberty to obtain a little temporary safety deserve neither liberty nor safety; for the essence of the series of decisions that year was that police, courts, and Congress itself had been systematically depriving Americans of the rights that the Declaration of Independence had called inalienable; and this was done in the name of security. A worse jolt was the discovery that our boasted superiority in the science of ballistics was a lot of hogwash, despite our terrific expenditures.

So if we are still a little punch-drunk perhaps we are coming out of it. But the fact that Macauley's cartoon of 1929 is still timely is no addition to the gaiety of the nation. The dead horse is there, and he has to be paid for. The American may have learned something in the past thirty years, but it is not to be denied that the figure in the background of the cartoon still represents him all too faithfully. Under the burden of the follies of the past, he still walks bow-legged.

Digression on the Man

Charles R. Macauley died only four years after receiving the Pulitzer Prize and is almost forgotten now, but for a time he was one of the most celebrated cartoonists in America. That was when he was working for the New York *World* and later for the Brooklyn *Eagle,* in both of which places he found an atmosphere congenial to his own temperament. It is a consideration given too little weight by laymen, although every cartoonist knows its importance.

Macauley's chief claim to fame is his invention of the Big Stick that he put into Theodore Roosevelt's hands. The incident is an admirable illustration of the cartoonist's function. The President, arguing for a national policy that a later generation calls "leading from strength," cited a maxim popular in the western cow country about 1885, when Roosevelt was on the range: "Speak softly and carry a big stick, and you will go far."

To the President it was a mere passing reference, but Macauley instantly saw its possibilities. The big stick he exaggerated into a club of such monstrous size that only the giant Fee-Fi-Fo-Fum could have wielded it; and that was what he put into Roosevelt's hands. It was so effective that it was adopted all over the country and eventually became the insigne of T. R. even more than the teeth and the eyeglasses.

9. An Old Struggle Still Going On

Edmund Duffy, 1931

I n 1931 Edmund Duffy made his first appearance in the list of Pulitzer Prize winners with a cartoon satirizing the Communist attack on religion. It is a good cartoon; yet as one looks back it is plain that the cartoonist, the subject and the date taken together provide a satirical flavor added by Time, not Duffy.

The cartoon was published in the Baltimore *Sun* of February 27, 1930, and the award was made in May, 1931. That is to say, the judges had had about nineteen months in which to make up their minds about the importance of events of October 1929. That was the month in which the bottom fell out of the stock market, a crash that was the prelude to the long depression that radically altered, and for a long time threatened to end, the American capitalistic economy.

One would think that comment on a catastrophe of such magnitude would take precedence over anything else that might be said by an observer of public affairs, but it was not so in 1931. On the contrary, upper-middle-class opinion tended to the view that realistic comment on the panic was in terribly bad taste, if not downright wicked. All that was lacking was confidence, said people of influence beginning with Herbert Hoover, President of the United States. If confidence could be restored, all would be well; and obviously confidence was not being restored by those raucous voices that were insisting upon a great deal more than a restoration of confidence.

In 1931 the mood of the class from which the advisory committee was drawn strikingly resembled the mood of the same

An Old Struggle Still Going On

Reproduced by permission of Edmund Duffy and the *Baltimore Sun*

class in the early days of 1958, when the economy was ailing again and another President was convinced that talking about its ailments would only make them worse. Hoover's repeated assertions that prosperity was just around the corner, and Eisenhower's invitation to the public to go into the market and buy—buy anything, but buy—were separated by twenty-seven years, but they were cut from the same cloth. Their similarity powerfully supports Hegel's observation that all we learn from history is that nations learn nothing from history.

Edmund Duffy drew better cartoons than this one in 1930, but his best were raucous comments on the increasing distress of the country. They were not designed to restore confidence. In the circumstances, therefore, it is not surprising that they were passed over and the one here presented chosen for the prize. Nevertheless, the fact is something of a satire on the country.

At the same time, the committee cannot fairly be accused of choosing a bad cartoon, either as regards craftsmanship, or as regards popular appeal. The drawing is fairly representative of Duffy's work in that it demonstrates his remarkable ability to convey the sense of energy. His figures even in repose are vibrant, and when they are in action it is immeasurably furious action. In this picture the effort of the Bolshevik is obviously futile. The cross bends, but one is certain that it will snap back into place the moment the physical force is released; and it is obvious that the assailant is already exerting his utmost strength—notice the feet, one having already lost purchase while the other is slipping. But how terrific is the sense of strain!

As for its appeal to the American public, one must bear in mind that this drawing was published in 1930, when many of the major crimes of the Communist regime in Russia were still unknown to most Americans. Trotzky, for example, although banished was not yet murdered, and the great blood-purge of the Old Bolsheviki was seven years ahead. The most ferociously cold-blooded iniquity of the Stalin regime, the deliberately planned starvation of two million peasants, was actually in process during the winter of 1929-30, but years were to pass before the American public learned the full extent of that atrocity.

The assualt on religion, however, was already common knowledge and in the eyes of Americans it had stamped the Soviet government with an infamy that holds in many minds to this day an evil eminence above all other crimes. It was this strong emotional charge that Duffy's cartoon touched, giving it an effectiveness in this country that no committee of judges could overlook, but that is incomprehensible to many foreigners, the Russians, no doubt, included.

We have formally and finally separated Church and State. We have forbidden Congress to make any law either establishing religion, or prohibiting its free exercise. A treaty negotiated in the time of President Washington—and treaties made under the Constitution rank with it as the supreme law of the land—is supposed to have contained the declaration, "The government of the United States is not, in any sense, founded on the Christian religion."

All this is taken as evidence that the American people are indifferent, not to say hostile, to religion. The truth that it relates only to an establishment of religion is incomprehensible to minds that can make no distinction between religion and the church. The capacity of Americans to make that distinction has concealed from the rest of the world the fact that they are among the most religious, or certainly the most pietistic peoples on earth. More than fifty per cent of the population today profess adherence to some formally organized religious sect, and they contribute, voluntarily, two billions a year to the maintenance of the churches.

It is true that this is no proof of any conspicuous holiness in the land. Many professing Christians, as the clergy constantly remind us with no small clamor, are Laodicean, "neither hot nor cold," in the faith. But it is also true that your rather indifferent churchman is often the very man who most furiously resents any disrespect to the forms of religion.

Hence the Communist assault on "the opiate of the people" made such an impression in the United States that many of its citizens, even after forty years, are unable to speak of "Communism," plain; they are under a psychological compulsion to precede it with "atheistic" or "godless," much as the traditional Unreconstructed Rebel in the South employed "damnyankee" as one word.

Any man who can tap such a wellspring of popular emotion is bound to produce an effect, usually a spectacular effect. In this cartoon Duffy accomplished it. The committee, required to give much weight to its popular effectiveness in judging a cartoonist's work, made no mistake in assuming that this one hit hard.

At the same time, one suspects that the committee felt no small relief at finding Duffy for once swinging his sledge hammer against a target that would emit no sparks of controversy. For 1930 was a time to sing low about the things that were really harassing the country. Confidence must not be disturbed, and blasting godless Communism would do nothing to shake the faith that prosperity was just around the corner and all would be well if the public would just go out into the market and buy.

Digression on the Man

Edmund Duffy, born in New Jersey in 1899, is a product of the Art Students' League and was strongly influenced by Boardman Robinson, a great cartoonist, but even greater as a teacher of cartoonists. He began his career as an illustrator and his work appeared in nearly every illustrated magazine of any importance prior to 1923 in which year he turned to political cartooning for the New York *Leader.* The next year he was brought to Baltimore by the *Sun,* to serve, tradition has it, for the three months of the Presidential campaign. He stayed twenty-four years, for a large part of the time turning out seven cartoons a week, and winning the Pulitzer Prize three times. In 1948 he went to *The Saturday Evening Post,* and later took up free-lance work.

Duffy admired the work of Rollin Kirby, but his only obvious borrowing from that master was the figure of Prohibition which, indeed, was borrowed by practically every cartoonist in the country, since it was one of those strokes of genius that say all there is to say. But aside from that one instance, he excelled Kirby when it was a question of exposing hypocrisy or, especially, stupidity. Duffy's pictures of the Ku Klux Klansman are as ruthless as Daumier or Goya.

But we shall meet him again, so enough for the moment.

10. A Wise Economist
Asks a Question

John T. McCutcheon, 1932

J
ohn T. McCutcheon, winner in 1932 for a cartoon published by the Chicago *Tribune* in 1931, was for the most part a cheerful philosopher. Although he spent his working life in the second largest city in the country, his work was more expressive of the small town and the farm than of the great centers of population. The Hannibal, Missouri, of Mark Twain's boyhood seemed to have influenced him more than the Chicago in which he spent his working life; but he was effective because a large proportion of the population of Chicago had come to the city from some place more or less like Hannibal.

McCutcheon was representative of the typical American small-towner of his generation in that superficially he was a realist, but fundamentally an idealist, and for most of the time an optimist. He had an eagle eye for frauds, and he laughed loudly at strutting pretense, especially when it donned the garb of righteousness; but basically he had a profound faith in what Theodore Roosevelt called "the old moralities" and he cherished no doubt that industry and thrift were cardinal virtues. To be exact, perhaps one should say that he had cherished no doubt until after 1929.

It is highly significant that this kind of man produced the bitterest cartoon that had won the Pulitzer Prize up to that date. "A Wise Economist Asks a Question," is the caption, the wise economist being a squirrel who asks a man on a park bench why he didn't save when times were good, and the answer is a simple, "I did."

The man is identified as a victim of bank failures and the background facts are that in 1931, the year this cartoon was published, 2,294 banks failed in this country, involving seventeen hundred millions of depositors' money, while at the same time unemployment reached eight millions, or 15.9 per cent of the total labor force. One able-bodied man in six could not find a job at the moment when the life savings of many were swept away in bank failures.

But those facts are statistical, and statistics furnish only a faint reflection of the real story. Twenty-seven years have passed, which means that a man must be forty years old today to have any accurate personal memory of the time, and it is doubtful that anyone can appreciate all that it means without personal experience of such a crisis; and there are only about sixty-five million people in the country above the age of forty years. To the majority, therefore, this cartoon must remain in part a mystery.

It is not impossible, however, for the majority to gain some comprehension of its significance by taking into consideration all the facts. The most important is the fact that the financial catastrophe was only the beginning of the disaster. In October, 1929, when the stock market lost sixteen billion dollars in one day, the country was startled, but more curious than terrified. The initial impression of most people was that some unidentified scoundrels had been at work. Memory went back sixty years to the thimblerigging of Jim Fisk and Jay Gould and Daniel Drew, that had precipitated stock-market crashes in the past. It was the comfortable assumption that presently the rascals responsible would be caught and jailed, and then things would straighten out.

But weeks stretched into months and then into years. No villains were identified as responsible, although many were accused, beginning with the hapless President, Herbert Hoover, and things didn't straighten out. The seasons followed their normal course, the sunshine and the rain did not fail, the harvests were prodigious, yet gaunt famine stalked the streets and the country roads, John Steinbeck's Okies began their dreary

A WISE ECONOMIST ASKS A QUESTION

pilgrimage from nowhere to nowhere, and despair settled like a fog over all the land.

McCutcheon's cartoon was drawn when this dismal process was just getting well under way, and it was still believed that bad banking practice was the chief trouble. But the man on the park bench has lost a great deal more than his money and his job; he has lost his faith in things that he had believed from youth up—in the efficacy of hard work and thrift to preserve a man from want, in the certainty of a reward for diligence and honesty, in the basic justice of the economic system, in the stability of the republic. All that he thought most solid and enduring has evaporated before his eyes and he is faced with the terror of vacuity, the one terror hardest for a man to beat down.

The money was a minor loss. Given half a chance he can make more money, but his utmost effort will never recover all the blithe confidence that was his heritage as an American boy.

There are subtleties in this picture that were to come out strongly a year or two later. The suggestion that economics is strictly for the squirrels was to become a dominant belief of millions within a few months. The pompous self-satisfaction of the animal figure is also prophetic. In 1931 many of the great lords of politics and finance were still clinging to the fatuous theory that they could talk the Depression out of existence, and they were uttering resounding idiocies every day. A year or so later some wit gathered the more sonorous ones into an anthology under the sardonic title, *Oh, Yeah?* that gave the country its first hearty laugh since 1929.

Students of public affairs are in fairly complete agreement that that year marks one of the great bends in the course of American history. The financial panic broke the fortunes of many men but—what was more important—it also broke the reputations of many pundits. The noun, "banker," in 1928 a cachet of respectability, by 1933 had become an epithet; but what suffered worst of all was the noun, "progress." The banker has slowly regained, not indeed his former sacro-sanctity, but at least a reputable status in society; but progress seems to have been permanently divested of its character as the inevitable destiny of America. Most Americans have regained faith in its possibility, but the old assurance of its inevitable triumph is gone forever.

A generation that did not witness this change may find it hard to credit its importance; but it was one of those "imponderables" that Bismarck said are sometimes more important to the destiny of nations than either political or military power. Its immediate effect was a striking transfer of confidence from the practical to the intellectual. The scholarship of the creator of the New Deal is, to be sure, but lightly esteemed by the learned societies; but if he seldom thought profoundly, his bitterest critics cannot deny that he thought fast, and he enlisted in his support an astonishing array of men who were scholarly beyond a doubt. Washington became infested with doctors of philosophy to an extent never before approached, and from that day to this, the professor in government service has been neither a scandal nor a curiosity, but a commonplace.

Many aver that the process was carried to a pernicious extreme; they say that in our consternation at the utter collapse of the practical engineer, we began to place in theorists a reliance that was even more dangerous, and for a quarter of a century they have battled consistently to reduce the intellectual to what they regard as his proper subordination to men who have met a payroll—and with some success.

However, through the Depression the government administered by eggheads did survive, and the shift from an economy of scarcity to an economy of abundance was made without complete disaster. A change so profound accomplished without political revolution is a rarity in human history. From this the pragmatic American argues that since the treatment worked, it must have been correct.

Most of the ideas of the New Deal are now taken as matters of course, for we still hold that the proof of the pudding is the chewing of the bag.

DIGRESSION ON THE MAN

Two McCutcheon brothers were part of that cultural explosion that made the sky luminous over Chicago from, say, *The Sultan of Sulu* to *Abraham Lincoln: The War Years,* that is, from the young George Ade to the old Carl Sandburg. Both the McCutcheons, John Tinney and George Barr, were as American as pumpkin pie, yet widely different. They worked both sides of the street. John Tinney, cartoonist, appealed to the side of American character that adored Huckleberry Finn; George Barr, novelist, appealed to the side that today adores Elizabeth II.

John Tinney brought into cartooning such features as the old swimmin' hole, the flop-eared dog and the barefoot boy, all parts of American sentimentality. George Barr brought into the novel the clean-cut young American who swept off her feet the Princess of Graustark, the other side of the same coin. From the Indiana farm on which they were born they went out and between them pretty well covered America.

John, indeed, pretty well covered the world. He joined the Navy and fought with Dewey at Manila Bay; he hunted big game with Theodore Roosevelt in Africa; and he was first to cross the Gobi Desert in an automobile—when the engine failed he rigged a sail of goatskins, and sailed the car the rest of the way. As an adventurer he outranks any other cartoonist in the list, and far surpassed the creations of his romantic brother's imagination.

Yet he could picture the American village of Bird Center more realistically than any other artist of his time. A man of parts, indeed.

11. The Light of Asia

H. M. Talburt, 1933

D oes anyone read Sir Edwin Arnold today? Matthew Arnold, yes, at least to the extent of a couple of lines describing that

> darkling plain
> Swept with confused alarms of struggle and flight,
> Where ignorant armies clash by night,

for in them Matthew made a singularly vivid forecast of the modern situation. But Edwin has faded until he is almost as dim a figure as that philosopher of history, Ibn Khaldun, whom Toynbee has read, but apparently nobody else.

Indeed his sun had set as long as twenty-five years ago; but among the literate there lingered enough of an afterglow to give familiarity to the phrase, "The Light of Asia." Many who had not read the book had seen or heard its title, and so could appreciate the sardonic element in its use as a caption for H. M. Talburt's winning cartoon in the year 1933. It had been published by the Washington *Daily News* on January 22, 1932.

But in a sense the cartoon is a plea for reconsideration of Edwin Arnold, although its immediate effect was nothing of the kind. It was popular because it was an attack on Japan, whose incendiary hand it portrayed carrying a torch made of the Kellogg Pact, a treaty by which nine nations, including Japan, had agreed to repudiate war "as an instrument of national policy." For his part in negotiating this treaty in 1928 the Nobel Peace Prize had been awarded to Frank B. Kellogg, the

American Secretary of State (whose name, by the way, Talburt misspelled).

A quarter of a century later there is no reason whatever to doubt the complete good faith of Frank Billings Kellogg, even though the younger generation may with some reason doubt his existence. But he did exist, and as the very model of a proper American citizen. Lawyer, Senator, Ambassador, and Secretary of State, he crowned his career as a judge of the High Court of International Justice, as lofty a position as a man of law could reach. Yet through the dust and smoke of recent years he is almost as hard to discern as Tiglath-pileser II, or the Senator from Virginia who is not Byrd.

The reason is that for all his high eminence he was essentially a fraud—not a hypocrite, mind you, and not a swindler, for he believed his own bunk, and his word was good; but nevertheless a fraud, for his beliefs *were* bunk, and the goods that he promised to deliver and, with great pains and labor, did deliver, were fustian. He died in 1937, doubtless convinced in his own mind that he had achieved greatly—to the end a fortunate man.

Yet to excoriate poor Kellogg for the emptiness of his diplomacy would be rank injustice. He was a man of his time and his time was one in which it is doubtful that Talleyrand, Disraeli, or Bismarck could have accomplished anything solid. Coolidge, that empty barrel, was President of the United States, and Baldwin, that empty hogshead, was Prime Minister of Great Britain. The French Foreign Minister with whom Kellogg negotiated was Aristide Briand, whose damning epitaph is, "He meant well."

History's condemnation of this group rests not on the fact that they did nothing, but on the fact that in all honesty they did not perceive the necessity of doing anything. Coolidge napped while the charges were being placed that would blow the economic system sky-high. Baldwin forced the abdication of an over-romantic king, but he did nothing to stop the Austrian corporal who was ten thousand times more dangerous than sentimental Edward. Briand fluttered and squawked like a hen who has hatched a clutch of duck-eggs and sees her progeny taking to water, but flutters and squawks were his limit.

Among them they produced the Kellogg Pact, by which

nine nations renounced war without doing anything effective to correct the conditions that were engendering war. Talburt, the cartoonist, was right—in Manchuria Japan put a match to the thing, which was a criminal act. But in all candor, what else can you do with a useless document?

The fatality that pursued these men was neither wickedness nor sloth. They were honest, as God gave them to see honesty, and most of them were industrious far beyond the average of their time. But every one of them—Briand perhaps excepted—had the imagination of a gatepost and "where there is no vision the people perish." The Kellogg Pact depended for its efficacy, not on the distribution of power as it existed in the contemporary world, but on the supposititious power of a promissory note. The mercantile minds of Baldwin and Kellogg were unable to imagine the existence of people to whom a signature was merely the scratch of a pen, with no more coercive effect than those Indian petroglyphs that no modern man can translate.

Edwin Arnold had known better, but in 1928 it was perhaps a psychological impossibility for the rulers of the world to take him seriously. He was thrice disqualified. He was a newspaper editor, which to practical men in 1928 meant that he had little sense. He was also a college professor, which meant that he had less sense. Finally, he was a poet, which meant that he had no sense at all. The proof of it was that in his book, *The Light of Asia,* he had written of Gautama the Buddha as if his heathenish ideas were to be compared seriously with True Religion.

As a matter of fact, Arnold was probably as sound a Christian as the Anglican Church could boast. But it cannot be denied that for five years he was a college professor in Bombay and he spent those years studying his pupils, not as interesting deviations from the norm of English schoolboys, but as a different species steeped in a philosophy of their own. A contemporary reader of *The Light of Asia* may suspect that Arnold was none too successful in understanding the Oriental mind, but at least he deemed it important to understand, and he made an effort.

In that he was miles ahead of the men who framed the Kellogg Pact and truly believed that in so doing they were erecting an impediment to war. It was, of course, the opposite. It was in the nature of a tranquilizing drug, reducing the peace-loving nations to apathy while the war-makers went about their work.

They could not be roused even by the reckless act of Japan in making a torch of the treaty. They could be only partially aroused when Hitler and Stalin clasped bloody hands, each holding a knife behind his back. The most apathetic of them all, the United States, was thoroughly aroused only when the bombs fell on Pearl Harbor, by which time it was years too late.

We fought our way out of the pitfall only at tremendous cost in blood and treasure, and what we finally reached was the same kind of uneasy peace that prevailed when Talburt drew his cartoon. Perhaps we understand Asia better than we did in those days, but that is by no means certain; some of the evidence points the other way. Our ten years' insistence that the island of Formosa is China, and the Red government of the mainland is only a passing fantasy of subversive persons, does not indicate that our study of the subject has been serious.

We do have much less confidence in scraps of paper than Secretary Kellogg had. The American bombers poised for instant flight clear across the world are something more than mere words. Nevertheless, when someone ventures to avow lack of confidence in Mr. Dulles' theory that the real Light of Asia is the Westminster Catechism, we hale him before the Un-American Activities Committee to be baited by a ring of Congressmen.

DIGRESSION ON THE MAN

Harold M. Talburt's journalistic career proceeded from writing to drawing. He broke into the craft by way of high-school reporting for the *News-Bee* in his native Toledo, Ohio, his energy in digging up stories acquiring him a place on the full-time staff. He made good as a writer, but the story goes that through the years when he was making his living with words he filled countless wastebaskets with pictorial ideas. Finally, an observant publisher transferred him from the typewriter to the drawing board.

When the Scripps-Howard chain needed a cartoonist in Washington in 1922 they chose Talburt, not altogether, it is safe to say, on account of his excellent draftsmanship. A cartoonist who has served time as a reporter, and who has become a good reporter, is usually equipped with a self-starter; that is to say, he can dig up an idea, as well as draw it. Such a cartoonist is God's gift to a chief editorial writer, who is usually put to it to feed verbal ideas to his writing staff, without having to furnish visual ones to the cartoonist as well.

For a newspaper chain the Washington assignment is of immense importance because the member papers look to it; and by the same token, the Washington cartoonist of a chain has an enormously expanded influence. He pays for it, however, by being restricted to national affairs, for it is frequently on some local issue that the man with the pencil can produce an impact like that of Nast on the local issue of the Tweed Ring.

12. California Points with Pride—!

Edmund Duffy, 1934

n 1933 the state of California was disgraced by a pair of lynchings and Governor James Rolph, Jr., made the mistake of trying to extenuate the crimes. The terrific riposte of Edmund Duffy, in the Baltimore *Sun,* brought him his second Pulitzer Prize in 1934.

"California Points With Pride" was technically unjust; if anybody pointed with pride it was Governor Rolph, but on the legal maxim that a principal is responsible for the acts of his agent, the state had earned this sting.

Yet there had been a good deal in the previous career of "Sunny Jim" to justify the voters in raising him to the highest office in the state. He was Mayor of San Francisco for nineteen years, and for at least fifteen years an excellent mayor, honest, energetic, constructive, and moderately liberal in his views. His seems to have been the case of a man of definite but limited ability for whom his job got too big. His administration of the city deteriorated during his last years, and in the governorship he was a catastrophic failure.

It must be admitted that he played in bad luck. The panic of 1929 wrecked the shipping business that had brought him a private fortune that made him independent of his salary as mayor. At the same time it enormously complicated the task of all government officials, even mayors, and the complication intensified as one went up the scale. When Rolph assumed the governorship in 1931 he took over a job calling for tremendous resourcefulness, imagination and courage; the last-named quality he had, but his resourcefulness and imagination were gone with his lost youth and his lost fortune. He was in trouble from the start, and died before the end of his term.

All moral considerations aside, his impulse to make excuses for lynchers in 1933 betrayed his inability to adjust his thinking to the times. California had been pretty rough in the early days, but the tradition of the Vigilantes had faded out and since 1882, when Tuskegee Institute began keeping a careful record, there had been only forty-one lynchings in the state up to the time of Rolph. For decades no public official, however barbarous his private inclinations, had dreamed of condoning the crime publicly. Rolph was forty years behind the times.

Lynching is a phenomenon so baldly inconsistent with a high level of civilization that its existence in the United States has puzzled foreign observers and for that matter drawn from native Americans more confusion and incoherence than rational analysis. It is only recently that we have begun to recognize it as primarily a symptom of defective social organization.

Laymen tend to forget that lynching is a crime unknown to the law. The law knows murder, and conspiracy to commit murder, but it does not and cannot recognize lynching as a distinct crime, for to do so would be to admit a defect in the operation of the law, thereby impairing its authority. Lynching had its origin in the fact that in certain areas at certain times the law did not operate with the speed and certainty required for the reasonable protection of society. The worse organized the society, the more difficult it is for the law to operate; and it is in a disorganized, or badly organized society that lynching flourishes—in California after 1849, in the late Confederacy after 1865, in Wyoming after the homesteaders became a serious annoyance to the cattlemen, leading to the "Johnson County War" of 1892.

The most spectacular example, of course, was furnished by the South after the destruction of the Confederacy, for there society remained badly disorganized for thirty-five years, owing to the imposition of peace terms that Southerners were no more inclined to meet than the Germans were inclined to meet those of 1919. As terms of compliance were gradually worked out, the practice declined, until in the years 1952, 1953 and 1954 it disappeared throughout the United States. But the social order was again upset by the Supreme Court decision re-

Reproduced by permission of Edmund Duffy and the *Baltimore Sun*

garding segregated schools in 1954, and 1955 had three lynchings.

Lynching is murder done, ostensibly at least, in the public rather than in a private interest. The law cannot admit any such distinction, but public opinion can and does. The effective argument against lynching is that it is unnecessary because due process of law is sufficient to take care of wrongs that infuriate and terrify the community; but when the law is patently unable to do anything of the kind, the mob will take over as it did in California in the old days. Whether it operates frankly as a mob, or under the name of Vigilantes, or Ku Klux, or Night Riders is a detail of no importance.

The remedy, of course, is worse than the disease, but the way to avoid the remedy is to eliminate the disease, which is lack of public confidence in legal justice. Unfortunately, what is one man's justice is another man's tyranny or, to put it with more precision, what is accepted as even-handed justice in one jurisdiction is regarded as outrageous oppression in another. Since the United States covers a vast number of vastly different local jurisdictions, any law applying to all is pretty sure to be resented in some.

But none of this bears on Duffy's cartoon. Take it any way you will, lynching is evidence of barbarism in the community in which it occurs. If apologists claim that the outbreak was due to intolerable wrongs, the community is none the less barbarous, because in a civilized society the law is able to put down intolerable wrongs. Owen Wister's smug pronouncement in *The Virginian* that the South lynched because it was semi-barbarous, but Wyoming lynched because it was determined to become civilized, was as rank a bit of casuistry as ever appeared in American literature. Both regions resorted to mob-murder because the law had broken down; and a community in which the law has broken down has reverted to barbarism, no matter at which point of the compass it lies.

The law breaks down whenever and wherever a majority of honest men can no longer believe in its efficacy as the protector of their lives, liberty, and property. Any effort to condone lynching is an admission that the breakdown has occurred, therefore it carries a more dreadful significance than the act of violence itself; Governor Rolph shocked the country more than the lynchers did, for murder can happen anywhere, but exculpation of murderers by officers of the law is possible only in the presence of social gangrene.

This much was generally accepted in 1934, as it is today. But that we have drawn the obvious inference, even after twenty-four years, is by no means certain. That inference is that the law must be consonant with the sense of justice of the majority of honest men. In theory we accept it, but in practice a good many of us are committed to the opposite view, namely, that the sense of justice of honest men must be consonant with the law, especially if it is a law to which we have given approval.

Hence comes a multiplication of laws to which many honest men cannot give approval; and when honest men see no justice in some laws, dishonest men take advantage of the fact to blaspheme against all law, even the law against murder, as an obscene farce, and lynching follows. The appearance of lynching in any state is presumptive evidence that the law in that state is in some respects rotten; and an extenuation of lynching is an admission of the charge.

Rolph, in effect, pleaded guilty for California; and a governor who does that is worse than maleficent, he is comic. A state may endure, at least for some time, a villainous chief executive, but none can tolerate a clown.

Digression on the Man

The charge that detraction has most frequently and most persistently brought against Edmund Duffy is that he has wit but no humor; but no true bill on this count was ever voted by those familiar with the man as well as his work.

He is an Irishman, which is to say he has an immense capacity for hatred, but his hatred does not rise to incandescence except when it is turned upon injustice. Duffy has also a towering capacity for contempt, which gives his thrusts a reach that mere hatred could never attain. This, of course, has won him more resentment than any other characteristic, for strong characters who are blandly indifferent to hatred cannot stand being spurned.

93

The quality that linked him to the masses during his long service on the Baltimore *Sun,* however, was not his ruthlessness, but his wild delight whenever Pomposity stepped on a banana peel and spilled itself all over the landscape. A terror to the unjust, he was utter ruin to frauds.

But the man who can laugh is also the man who can mourn. On the morning after the surrender of Corregidor, Duffy had a cartoon called after Steinbeck, *The Moon Is Down,* a drawing whose stark simplicity carried woe unutterable. In short, he is a cartoonist, not an identification-tag distributor.

13. Sure, I'll Work for Both Sides

Ross A. Lewis, 1935

T he prize-winning cartoon for 1935, by Ross Lewis, of the Milwaukee *Journal*, has a special interest for the very reason that in the light of 1958 it seems inane. "Sure, I'll Work for Both Sides," is the caption of a picture showing a giant marked "Violence" with a foot on each side of the fence between industry and strikers.

Certainly violence has been employed by both labor and management in industrial disputes. Everybody knows that, so why mention it? Especially why give a man a Pulitzer Prize for mentioning it? In 1958 the cartoon would have more point if the giant were labeled "Corruption," for it has been amply demonstrated that nowadays bribery, theft, perjury and betrayal of trust also work for both sides. In retrospect the man who threw a cobblestone in 1935 seems almost innocent by comparison with the modern crooks who neatly sell out the employers to the union in one place and in the next sell out the union to the employers.

But this drawing was published in 1934 and much water has flowed under the bridge since then. In 1934 the Depression had just passed its lowest point. The official figure for unemployment in 1934 was 11,340,000, or 21.7 per cent of the total labor force, and most men were convinced that the government statisticians were holding the figure as low as they could without complete self-stultification. It had been a little worse in the previous year, but the recovery in employment was only about three percentage points—24.9 per cent to 21.7—and at that rate men figured that while prosperity might eventually

95

come back, most of those concerned would be dead, or at least senile before it returned. Hope was, as the market reporters delicately put it, in short supply.

In 1934 apathy had settled upon the country to an extent that is now hard to believe. True, there was tremendous intellectual ferment in Washington, but not until the next year, 1935, did it begin to percolate down to the masses. At the moment when Lewis' cartoon was published millions of Americans were inert, dazed by the calamity that had overtaken them and not disposed to move in any direction.

Even to a dull mind this was abnormal, and to an alert mind it was sinister. For three hundred and twenty-seven years, ever since Capt. John Smith compelled the gentlemen at Jamestown to pick up their hoes and repair to the cornfield, Americans had been exhibiting enormous capacity for practically anything in the world except sitting still. Now they were sitting still, and it was completely out of character.

Nobody believed it would last, or could last. Eventually the people would go into action, but what kind of action? There, as Hamlet put it with visions of hell before him, was the rub. Fifteen years earlier Americans, organized into a disciplined force, had proved very effectively violent on European battlefields. It stood to reason that the same energy in an indisciplined mob might be effective at home, perhaps dreadfully effective.

There had, indeed, already been a taste of it. In 1932, before the people had been completely numbed by the collapse of the banking system, things were getting out of hand. In the Middle West, long regarded as the strong fortress of solid Americanism, troops had to be called out to repress desperate milk farmers, while mobs of corn and wheat farmers had pulled judges off the bench and terrorized sheriffs to prevent sales of property by foreclosure. In early 1933 the crash of the banking system had paralyzed even the mobs, but it was obvious that the inaction was temporary. One of two things was inevitable: the people were going to work, or they were going to riot.

What happened, of course, was that they went to work—slowly, with much fumbling, many false starts, considerable waste, and a terrific clamor of contradictory advice, vilification and abuse but, on the whole, fairly steadily. The capitalistic

SURE, I'LL WORK FOR BOTH SIDES

system and representative democracy survived.

But that is hindsight. In 1934, when Lewis drew his cartoon, nobody knew what was ahead. In 1934 it seemed possible that anything might happen, not excluding the collapse of the republic. Terrific examples were being furnished by the rest of the world. The full extent of Stalin's starvation of the peasants was just beginning to be known, and in June of that year Adolf Hitler staged the first of his blood purges, when more than a thousand victims, of types all the way from the infamous Roehm to the honorable Von Schleicher and his completely innocent wife, were murdered in one night of horror.

Obviously, the boasted civilization of the west was a thin crust over a volcano of barbarism, at least in Germany and Russia. Who could say that it was appreciably thicker in the United States? It was a question without an answer in 1934. For that matter, to this day we cannot measure exactly the margin by which we escaped an appalling upheaval; but there is plenty of evidence that the margin was none too wide.

Violence was in the air in 1934 and all men knew it. What nobody knew with certainty was the most effective method of preventing its precipitation from a brooding presence in the atmosphere into overt action in the streets. Every measure adopted to that end was denounced as ill-chosen, and many were branded as incitements to the very disorders they were supposed to prevent. The quarrel was long ago transformed into a war of words among the historians, but it still rages and doubtless will continue for many years to come.

All that can be said with assurance twenty-four years later is that the crisis passed without ruinous damage to the American social structure. Whether its passing was hastened or delayed by the radical modifications then made in the political and economic structure may be open to debate; although since the country did survive the burden of proof would seem to rest on the prosecution, rather than on the defense.

In any event, the American of 1958 can look back on that episode in our national history with some degree of satisfaction. If he approves, on the whole, of the changes effected at the time, he may draw the pleasing inference that American political genius proved adequate to deal with a crisis that wrecked more than half the governments of the western world. On the other hand, if he disapproves of what was done then, he may comfort himself with the reflection that the American system proved resilient enough to triumph over folly within as well as assault from without.

But in neither case should he jump to the conclusion that, because Lewis' cartoon seems an inanity today, therefore the men who awarded it the prize must have been dull fellows, insensitive to what was taking place around them. True, they were skittish about taking either side in the great debate then raging; they had no mind to "fright the ladies" and so come in danger of being hanged, but they knew very well that fear of a Reign of Terror was the sorest spot in contemporary America and they knew that this cartoon touched it.

When your probe reaches an inflamed nerve, the thrust may be described by any number of epithets, but you cannot call it ineffective.

DIGRESSION ON THE MAN

If the discerning critic detects a hint of the vigorous line of Boardman Robinson in this cartoon, there is no mystery about it, for Ross A. Lewis, a native of Michigan, studied under Robinson and Walter Jack Duncan at the Art Students' League in New York, where he had gone from Milwaukee State College and the Layton School of Art in Milwaukee.

From the school he went for three years into what painters, etchers and cartoonists agree is the villein socage ("services not of an honorable nature," says Webster) of the art world, the illustration of advertisements. Nevertheless, this commercial art is not only an effective means of keeping the wolf from the door, but it must be a fairly good training-ground for cartoonists, since an impressive number of the ablest have been through that mill.

In any event, Lewis soon demonstrated that his aptitude was more journalistic than mercantile, and by 1932 he was installed as full-time cartoonist for the editorial page of the Milwaukee *Journal,* and within three years he had brought the distinction of the Pulitzer Prize to that newspaper. Fast work indeed for one who was a lowly decorator of ads so short a time before.

14. Come on in, I'll treat you right. I used to know your Daddy

C. D. Batchelor, 1937

For reasons undisclosed and not germane to this inquiry no award was made in 1936, but in 1937 the judges handed down a decision that for once carries no suggestion of Nice-Nellyism. The winner was C. D. Batchelor, of the New York *Daily News,* and his cartoon was the wickedest, bitterest, and perhaps the most brilliant in the whole series.

A prostitute whose face is a death's-head and whose name is War, stands in her doorway and says to Any European Youth, "Come on in. I'll treat you right. I used to know your daddy." Behind her a poster stuck on the wall advertises, "Follies of 1936. Starring Hitler, Mussolini, Stalin."

It is brutal—as brutal as the words of Proverbs, 5:5, "Her feet go down to death; her steps take hold on hell"; as brutal as truth.

The salvation of this cartoon is the face of the young man. Logically, Batchelor might have drawn a simpleton, and by so doing he would have followed the line of the writer of Proverbs. Instead, he made the face a fine one, intelligent and attractive, thereby injecting pity into the composition and lifting it above the level of the brute.

In the year that this cartoon was published many thousands of the men who held Pershing's line on November 11, 1918, were just touching the height of their intellectual power and professional skills; but the passage of eighteen years had not

COME ON IN, I'LL TREAT YOU RIGHT. I USED TO
KNOW YOUR DADDY

erased their memory of the obscenity of war as the man on active service in the field sees it. Many of them were heads of families, with sons approaching the age of military service; the timing was perfect.

And the timing is perfect again. The men who were commanded by Eisenhower and MacArthur are, in 1958, nearly in the position, in 1936, of those who were commanded by Pershing. They are thirteen years older than they were when they made the acquaintance of War. They have sons at, or approaching, adolescence, which is to say, eligible for the next world war; and Dad, who knew the old whore between 1941 and 1945, turns sick at his stomach when he thinks that she may soon be in business again.

But Batchelor had more than an audience specially prepared by its own experience to appreciate the full force of his cartoon. He had a still larger audience conditioned, not by personal service, but by the traditions and philosophy of many generations. This drawing reflects the attitude, not of veterans only, but of the American people generally.

It is a nonmilitaristic nation, which may go far to explain why it has never lost a war. The Man on Horseback has never appealed to enough Americans to become dangerous—a considered opinion not shaken by the immense popularity of Washington, Jackson, Grant, and Eisenhower. In the first place, neither Washington nor Jackson was a professional soldier, and in the second place neither Grant nor Eisenhower was a spit-and-polish soldier. Each took a decent pride in his honorable record, of course, but neither had any patience with the pursuit of glory for its own sake, nor much faith in military trappings as supporters of morale.

The American soldier has always gone into battle for the one purpose of killing the enemy as expeditiously and conveniently as may be. It is a dirty job, to be disposed of with all possible speed, and the man who exults in it is regarded, even by his comrades-in-arms, as a preposterous ass. Certain German military observers during the Second World War commented scornfully on the fact that advancing American infantry at the first burst of machine-gun fire hit the dirt and yelled for the tanks. That, thought the Germans, was not military virtue.

Perhaps it was not, but it had great survival value. It tended to bring about a situation in which a great many American infantrymen were alive, while most of the Germans were dead; which is the situation that the Americans were there to bring about. They were not out to win glory, they were out to win the war. And they won it.

American disdain of every effort to prettify war is illustrated by the American military uniform. After 1865 we had thirty-three years of peace in the course of which the dress of the American soldier became gaudier and gaudier. Then came the brush with Spain, which proved that blue cloth and brass buttons made an excellent target for high-powered rifles, so we took to khaki. World War I finished choker collars and puttees. World War II, quickly followed by the Korean affair, finished everything else that could hamper a man's movements. Today the private soldier of the United States looks, except on ceremonial occasions, more like a garbage collector than like the traditional military man.

And why not? His business is to fight, not to impress the girls. Above all, it is not his business to provide a setting so gorgeous that the central figure in it will seem to the thoughtless no longer a man, but the possessor of some of the attributes of divinity, that is to say, a king. The American Army is not designed to be the showpiece at a coronation, still less at anything like the extravaganzas that Hitler once staged at Nuremberg. It is designed solely to administer grief to any armed enemy of the country; which it has done with marked success, so far.

It is a question, however, that this attitude can survive the emergence of the republic as one of the two super-powers bestriding the world. Colossal power is highly intoxicating. Even more than alcohol, it is destructive of common sense and it takes a very hard head to stand it.

To date Americans have been sufficiently hard-headed, but hitherto we had swallowed no such tremendous draughts as we have been imbibing since 1945. Ruthless necessity has compelled us to create a gigantic military establishment; it remains to be seen whether or not that will be followed by establishment of a military caste. The services for the first time offer an attractive career to more than a mere handful of able officers; powerful minds are no longer being forced out by the lack of all hope of promotion, and are remaining in the life. In another generation there may be enough of them to form a really powerful faction.

This is a possibility that cannot be disregarded by any serious student of public affairs; nor can it be regarded with entire equanimity. Militarism in the nature of the case implies some toleration of war. The award to Batchelor is evidence that up to 1937 American opinion held this in the same distaste that it held for what the French discreetly term the "tolerated house." But nearly twenty years have passed; has the trend in that time been toward allowing a quasi-respectability to an institution formerly regarded with loathing? Are we beginning to feel an inclination to look upon the old trollop as no longer a harlot, but as a *demimondaine,* which is halfway toward making her an honest woman?

It is a question that every American voter must answer somehow, for tacit acquiescence is an answer. But aside from that, here is a great cartoon that is as well worth studying today as it was when it was first published. If you doubt it, consider how well it is described by a reversal of the cigarette manufacturer's slogan: There's *something* about it you'll dislike.

Digression on the Man

Clarence Daniel Batchelor is another product of the New York Art Students' League, reinforced this time by the Chicago Art Institute, which he attended first. He was born at Osage City, Kansas, in 1888, and it is his habit to insist that the date of the event was highly appropriate for the cartoonist—April 1, All Fools' Day.

But if his career has been marked by folly outside observers cannot detect it. He worked briefly for the Kansas City *Star,* free-lanced for a while, spent six years with the New York *Journal* and ten with a syndicate until he was annexed by the enormously popular *Daily News.* His was the distinction of dragging down the first Pulitzer Prize awarded to a tabloid.

Batchelor first built up his reputation as a social, rather than a political, satirist. His campaign against slaughter on the highways, a series run under the general title "Inviting the Undertaker," spread far beyond New York because of its remarkable understanding of the insanities of the nut behind the wheel. Every drawing in that series was uncomfortably familiar to the average driver; if he hadn't been guilty of the folly described, he had seen it often enough to recognize it instantly.

Batchelor's attitude, in brief, is like that toward sin of the preacher Coolidge heard—the cartoonist preaches about death, and he is against it.

15. The Road Back

Vaughn Shoemaker, 1938

O n Armistice Day, 1937, the Chicago *Daily News* published a cartoon by Vaughan Shoemaker which was awarded the prize in 1938. It is a picture of a man going backward, but twenty years later it may be plausibly argued that the whole cartoon is in reverse. In the drawing a soldier, French to judge by his uniform, plods doggedly past Milestone 1937 toward Milestone 1936 and beyond that toward a distant conflagration labeled "World War," while a horrified world cries, "You're going the wrong way!"

In the light of 1958 two errors in this presentation are glaringly conspicuous. The first is that it shows a soldier going back while a shocked world protests; we know now that it was the world that was going back while shocked soldiers protested. The second is that the conflagration is named simply "World War," which was deemed adequate at the time, but which we know now was tragically wrong. The correct appellation is "World War I."

It was precisely in the year 1937 that the post-war policy of the United States touched the apex of its folly in the Neurality Act of that year and the Ludlow Resolution. The Neutrality Act was passed in July and the resolution was introduced in December; but by the time the vote was reached, after the new year had come in, the high tide of folly had receded and the resolution was beaten in the House, 209-188.

These efforts are described merely as the policy, not the foreign policy, of the country. Both were efforts to take foreign

THE ROAD BACK?

policy out of the hands of the executive, to which the Constitution had consigned it, and place it elsewhere. The Neutrality Act deprived the President of discretion in the matter of selling arms to belligerents. The Ludlow Resolution would have deprived Congress itself of the power to declare war, and would have substituted the lunatic procedure of a popular referendum.

The Neutrality Act made it impossible for us to render aid to the Spanish Republic, but did not prevent Franco from getting ample aid from Hitler and Mussolini. So the Republic turned for help to Soviet Russia and, as usual, Communist aid proved disastrous. The act made it difficult for us to render aid to China against Japan, so China was overrun and in the end the Chinese masses, too, were persuaded that their only friends in the outside world were the Communists.

It all stemmed from the original error of 1919, when we allowed foreign policy to become the football of partisan politics. Woodrow Wilson returned from Paris with what seemed to be a feasible scheme of collective security. It was rejected, but there is reason to believe that many of the men who rejected it, including the leader of the opposition, Senator Lodge the elder, did not intend the rejection to be final and irrevocable. They meant no more than to postpone the arrangement until after the election of 1920, when they hoped that their own party would come into power and secure the credit for making a satisfactory peace.

But to justify even a temporary rejection it was deemed necessary to convince the people that their President had played them false by signing a viciously bad treaty. This they accomplished; but, having once conjured up the Devil of suspicion and hate, they could not control him. The party did win the election of 1920, but the technique of misrepresentation had succeeded so well that it was impossible to undo the work and bring the United States into line with the best thought of the civilized world.

Some fifteen years after 1919 Adolf Hitler flattered himself that he had invented the method of the Big Lie. He was a fool in that as in many other things. More adeptly than he ever used it, it had been used to demolish the first effort at collective security, thereby opening the way for dictators to achieve their monstrous careers.

But this was little understood in 1937; in fact it is not universally understood today. Many Americans in 1937 were, and some still are under the spell of the illusion created in 1919. The people had suffered grievously in the First World War and many honestly believed that the people never suffer from their own folly, but only when some villain has betrayed them.

There were others who, without accepting this nonsense for a moment, had a keen appreciation of its political value. Convince the believers that the villain they seek is the leader of the other party or, if your party is in power, the head of another branch of the government, and you can pose as their champion to enormous political profit.

Under this program the first villain was Wilson, and when he was disposed of, the next was the President, any President; and if the President happened to be such a nullity as Harding, then his advisers, especially the Secretary of State. After Wilson went down, Charles E. Hughes, in the State Department, became a shining target for the voodoo doctors, and even Herbert Hoover, at Commerce, came in for some of their delicate attentions.

In 1929 the Republican party was wrecked by the collapse of its economic policy, or lack of policy. But the wrath of the voters centered on domestic affairs. The myth of the wise and benevolent Captains of Industry and Finance busted with the boom, but the mythology of foreign relations survived. Collection of the old war debts, for example, was still considered feasible and failure to pay them was attributed to moral turpitude. It was this illusion that enabled Senator Hiram Johnson, of California, to put through his debt default act of 1937, forbidding the United States to lend money to foreign nations already in default, which meant our allies in the late war.

A parallel myth enabled Senator Gerald P. Nye, of North Dakota, to produce a tremendous effect with an investigation of the munitions industry. All that the investigation proved was that the munitions manufacturers had made huge profits, which everybody knew before the inquiry began. What it did not prove, but nevertheless established as an article of faith in millions of minds, was that the people who profited by the war must have caused it. There followed a series of so-called Neutrality Acts, designed to prevent war by preventing trade in munitions.

The effect, of course, was not to prevent war, but to convince the dictators, Hitler and Mussolini completely, and Stalin and the Japanese militarists halfway, that the foreign policy of the United States was dictated entirely by the profit motive. It followed that the American people would under no circumstances fight for a principle; so if it could be shown that no profit could be gained by fighting, the American republic would not lift a hand to prevent the grossest outrage.

In the end this error proved fatal to the dictators and extremely costly to the United States, but it was a natural one— a logical inference from the sort of politics we had played for seventeen years prior to 1937. The American will to believe that our sufferings were due to the combination of rascally debtors abroad and scoundrelly profiteers at home was too strong even for the greatest popular idol of the time. All the eloquence and skill of Franklin D. Roosevelt were not enough to prevent the passage of the acts, or to persuade us that a successful foreign policy depends at least as much on what aliens think of us as on what we think of aliens.

A majority learned it only after it had been hammered into us by the fearful double war of 1941-45; and some have not learned it yet. The bipartisan policy, that domestic politics ends at the water's edge, was established when Arthur H. Vandenberg, a Republican Senator from Michigan and the ablest leader of the isolationists, saw the light and brought his party into line—incidentally, gaining a permanent niche in history among true patriots.

Even so, the myths die hard. Truth is precious, and all that, but frequently a lie is much more comfortable, much easier to understand.

DIGRESSION ON THE MAN

Vaughn Shoemaker, another double-barreled prize-winner, will be merely identified here. He is strictly a Chicago product, born there in 1902, and doing his most important work for the *Daily News* of his native city, although he achieved a considerable success with the sidelines of lecturing and television work.

There is an anecdote concerning him, however, that deserves perpetuity. In his youth he was athletic enough to hold a job as lifeguard at a lakeside beach, but his muscular development and coordination made no impression on the teacher to whom he first applied for art lessons. After a considerable period of what must have been a severe struggle the teacher is reported to have said, "You'll never make a cartoonist. I am so sure of it that if you will quit now, I'll refund your money."

Addressed to a pupil who was to become one of the youngest chief cartoonists in the country and twice winner of the Pulitzer Prize, this remark should be embalmed in history.

16. Nomination for 1938

Charles G. Werner, 1939

The ghost of the Republic of Czechoslovakia is nearly if not quite the grisliest political spectre that memory conjures up before the American mind. The story of Czechoslovakia is more than the tragedy of a brave and admirable nation fallen; it is also a rough confutation of easy American optimism, and therefore still gives the thoughtful a twinge of terror.

The tragedy was commemorated in a cartoon by Charles G. Werner, published in the Oklahoma City *Oklahoman*, October 6, 1938, and awarded the Pulitzer Prize in 1939. Werner's proposal of dead Czechoslovakia for the Nobel Peace Prize undoubtedly reflected American opinion at the moment; but it hardly touches an element in that opinion that has been increasing in importance for the past twenty years.

The historical episode of the rise and fall of Czechoslovakia was a savage demonstration that we live in a world in which right is not might, and a rational and civilized polity is a poor guarantee of survival. Yet if these things are not basically vital there is no sense in the second paragraph of the Declaration of Independence, nor in the preamble to the Consitution of the United States. They are both based on the assumption that there is power in intelligence and a fair assurance of safety in reasonable conduct.

Czechoslovakia was, in the minds of most Americans, a model exemplification of both qualities. The two Masaryks and Eduard Beneš were statesmen whose ideas we could understand, and the financial and industrial leaders of the republic

NOMINATION FOR 1938

operated in a way we could understand. The rapid recovery of Czechoslovakia after 1918, its tremendous prosperity during the twenties, and its relative stability even in the dismal early thirties seemed to us to set an example that might convince the rest of Europe of the value of democratic freedom.

We chose to overlook the fact that a large part of Europe had come under the control of perverts. It was convenient to overlook it because the rise of these creatures had been assisted to no small extent by the defection of the United States in the matter of the League of Nations. It was possible to overlook it because while we knew, even in 1938, that they were wicked men we had at that time no idea of the full magnitude of their infamy. We knew little or nothing about Dachau and Oświęcim. We did not dream of the gas chambers and cremation ovens, or of the "scientific" experiments upon human beings. We hugged the delusion that nothing like Caligula could rule an empire in modern times, and when a few informed persons told us that by comparison with Adolf Hitler, Caligula was downright benevolent, we dismissed the assertion as fabulous.

Well, we know better now. Twenty years afterward the ghost of Czechoslovakia still walks the earth to remind us that reason and good-will excite terror in the hearts of evil men; and evil men are still plentiful and still strong. Reason and good-will in its polity are therefore grounds for destroying a nation, not for imitating it. They do, indeed, have power over the minds of men, irresistible power if they are given time to operate, so it is of prime importance to the evil to give them no time. Hitler was perfectly correct in his belief that the mere existence of Czechoslovakia would eventually spell his doom, and the doom of others like him. The extinction of the democratic republic was a necessity if Hitlerism were to survive.

In the end, of course, he encountered reason and good-will backed by strength and the resolution to use it; so in the end Hitler died under the ruins of his own flaming capital. But it was a near thing. The triumph came too late for Czechoslovakia, almost too late for France, in time for Britain by the narrowest of margins, and leaving even the United States shaken and deeply perturbed.

So the ghost walks and although, like Hamlet, we shift our ground, it haunts us still, *hic et ubique*. Hitler had been dead three years when the second Masaryk, Jan, went out of a window—defenestrated, men said, reviving an antique word to describe a crime that we had thought antiquated. But then we had thought that tyrants whose sport is murder were antiquated, too, only to find that the passage of the centuries has made them bloodier than Nero, or Attila, or Genghiz, and acquainted with refinements of torture unknown to the Iroquois.

Werner's suggestion that the Nobel Peace Prize for 1938 be dedicated to the memory of Czechoslovakia was not accepted. The prize went, instead, to the Nansen International Office for Refugees, at Geneva. That is to say, in 1938 the judges could find no one distinguished for his success in promoting peace, so they gave the award to an institution trying to mitigate the horrors of war—an acknowledgment of defeat.

In the twenty years that have followed, the award has been given only ten times, and three of the winners were humanitarian institutions—the Red Cross, the Friends Service Committee, and the United Nations Office for Refugees—which suggests that only thirty-five per cent of the time are any statesman's strivings for peace notably effective.

That is a biting commentary on something, but is that something the state of the modern world, or the idea of giving a peace prize? Another ghostly voice echoes an answer to that question, the voice not of a dead nation, but of a dead American: "Is life so dear, or peace so sweet, as to be purchased at the price of chains and slavery?" Patrick Henry never won or deserved a peace prize. It was obviously his opinion that peace, like happiness, is rarely attained by direct action; if it comes at all, it comes of itself, after the creation of conditions favorable to its existence.

But the creation of conditions favorable to peace involves bitter struggle, since the first of those conditions is substantial justice. More than two thousand years ago Socrates discovered that the hardest question men can try to answer is, What is just? It has not become any easier although a score of centuries have followed, bringing vast information about injustice. It is the irony of fate that as knowledge extends questions become harder, not easier, and most of the answers are visible only to hindsight.

Twenty years later it is as plain as the sun in heaven that we should have intervened to save Czechoslovakia. It would have been not only good morals, but good business, saving us money. We were foolish, and unfortunately it does not follow that we who were then foolish have now grown wise. It is not certain that we have mastered the all-important fact that it is not happiness, but only the pursuit of happiness that is an inalienable right of man; and like unto it is the pursuit of peace.

DIGRESSION ON THE MAN

Charles George Werner, native of Wisconsin, but beginning his newspaper career in Missouri, acknowledged no training except a few weeks' tutelage by Jay N. Darling. It is an unusual circumstance that after he had won the Pulitzer Prize he went to the Chicago Art Institute, where many prize-winners began.

Werner, born in 1909, at thirty was the youngest cartoonist to capture the prize and retain that distinction until Mauldin came along to displace him by winning at twenty-two.

Werner began as a photographer with the Springfield, Missouri, *Leader and Press,* but he was doing some drawing even then. Perhaps an art critic would attribute his careful attention to light in his drawing to his early experience with the camera. In any event, he transferred to the Oklahoma City *Oklahoman* as a member of the art department, and not until 1937 did he become an editorial page cartoonist. Some editor must have preened himself on his own judgment when, only a year later, the new cartoonist turned in a piece of work that won the Pulitzer Prize.

Later Werner went to the Chicago *Sun* and then to the Indianapolis *Star,* where he has been for a dozen years.

17. The Outstretched Hand

Edmund Duffy, 1940

E dmund Duffy took his third Pulitzer Prize in 1940 with "The Outstretched Hand," published in the Baltimore *Sun* the previous year. It is a satire upon Hitler's peace offers made at the moment when he, in collaboration with Stalin, was wrecking Poland. The outstretched hand drips blood, while the other hand clutches scraps of paper that were promises and solemn treaties. Smoking ruins supply the background.

A strong claim can be made for Duffy's pictures of Hitler as the most revolting produced by any American cartoonist. The effect is produced by a subtle contrast. Duffy is careful always to dress Hitler rather jauntily; the anthropoid element is confined to the face. The theory is that a well-tailored gorilla is more horrifying than one clad only in his own hair, and the theory is sound.

Hitler broke into Poland September 1, 1939, and simultaneously he broke the rose-colored spectacles through which millions of Americans had been viewing the operations of the dictators. It is true that years were still to pass before we should be able to see them clearly. The war was over before the full enormity of their acts was disclosed, but at least we endowed them with none of the trappings of heroes after September, 1939.

We had previously made every effort to do just that, with a considerable measure of success as regards Mussolini, with large success as regards Franco, and with some success even as regards Stalin. Hitler was more difficult to disguise because of

the four he was the most candid. *Mein Kampf* was rather too stiff a dose even for those Americans whose political theory was confined to loathing the memory of Woodrow Wilson and feeding that hate by lauding everything German.

Among such Americans the accepted method of dealing with that amazing record of butchery was simply not to read it, and to refuse belief when others quoted it. In May, 1939, Senator Borah, who had ranked as a chief among the assassins of the League of Nations, insolently accused the Secretary of State of being an ignoramus; to his face the Senator told him that the Secretary's information was worthless and that he, Borah, knew that there would be no war in 1939.

It is possible that Borah was goaded into this folly by a sense of his own responsibility for the course that events had taken; but there is no doubt that he represented a large segment of public opinion. Some of it certainly was pacifist opinion; but a great deal of it was the opinion of those who hate blood, toil, tears and sweat more than they cherish "a decent respect to the opinions of mankind." Love of peace is not to be equated with dread of the risks and labors of war, even though they frequently work toward the same end.

In any event, the Duffy cartoon of 1939 accurately reflected the state of mind of nearly all Americans at that date. The stunning factor was not the emergence of a monster, for that had many precedents, but the fact that this monster wore the garb of a civilized man. It was more than the polished boots and the Sam Browne belt. The man also appreciated not, indeed, the spirit, but the high utility of science and art. If an Australian Bushman acted like a savage in 1939 it was no more than we expected. Even a shaggy Bolshevik, commonly conceived as bristling with whiskers and in deathly fear of soap, could play the barbarian without shattering our sense of the fitness of things.

But here was a man who was the heir of a great civilization, a man who could talk, not altogether idiotically, of the music of Wagner, a man who could command the loyalty of scientists and scholars at least of the second class, and of soldiers and industrialists of the first class—yet a man capable of devising and perpetrating atrocities of a kind that we thought had gone out with cannibalism. Hitler as an individual appalled us;

Reproduced by permission of Edmund Duffy and the *Baltimore Sun*

but Hitler as a revelation of the fragility of civilization well-nigh paralyzed us.

This was the period of the so-called "phony war," which was really a temporary paralysis of the will among the western democracies. It was a stupor from which France did not recover in time, and Britain barely in the nick of time, while the United States was not shaken out of it until the jolt of Pearl Harbor, two years later.

It was the paralysis of terror, all right, but not of physical fear. France, for example, was far more afraid of the military power of Wilhelm II in 1914 than she was of Hitler's in 1939; yet against the supposedly irresistible might of imperial Germany the French Army fought with a brilliance that added to the lustre of its days of greatest glory, while against Hitler it fought feebly and soon collapsed.

The difference was that in 1939 the French were facing something that they did not understand. Power, including the most ruthless power, they understood perfectly; and power was what they faced in 1914. But diabolism they did not understand. Tanks and infantry and airpower are creations of man's ingenuity, and with equal ingenuity they can be successfully resisted. But the horde that burst into France in 1940 was inspired by something for which the French have a name, but little comprehension; they call it a *mystique*. As probably the most severely rational nation on earth, when they encounter a really powerful *mystique* the French are beyond their depth; and that applies, whether the *mystique* in question derives from heaven or from hell.

Military post-mortems have revealed that the French common soldier acquitted himself very well in 1940; but it is never the common soldier who is most affected by the imponderables in war. It is the high command, and it was the high command that failed in France, not through cowardice or imbecility, but through sheer inability to believe its own eyes.

Before we visit unsparing condemnation on the French generals, let us consider how desperately close we came to doing the same thing. Borah in May preceding that explosive September knew there would be no war. The House of Representatives in midsummer that year came within one vote of passing a bill disbanding a large part of the Army. Right to the end General MacArthur continued to believe that Japan was the important enemy, and that what happened in Europe was a sideshow that should have received secondary attention until after Japan had been defeated.

The sober truth is that contemplation of 1939 tends to sustain the contention of the old-fashioned theologians, one of whom stated the principle with admirable economy of words as, "When hell drops out of religion, justice drops out of politics." By 1939 we were pretty well convinced that war grew out of economic conditions exclusively and that the concept of hell, that is, of absolute evil, was an aberration of fundamentalist evangelists. Duffy showed us with photographic precision the Devil rising from the Bottomless Pit; we admitted that it was a powerful cartoon, and gave it the prize; but for the rest, like the traditional farmer contemplating the circus giraffe, we turned aside, spat, and said, "There ain't no sich animal!"

DIGRESSION ON THE MAN

Having drawn abreast of the Old Master, Rollin Kirby, by winning three times, Duffy quit newspaper cartooning in 1948. He has done some work since for the weekly *Saturday Evening Post,* and various other journals, but he has been out of the heat and clamor of daily journalism.

For that he is not subject to just criticism, for he had put in twenty-four tremendously productive years on the Baltimore *Sun;* and after such service any man is eligible for honorable retirement.

Nevertheless, his withdrawal was a loss to journalism for he was one of the relatively few who, accepting and discharging the duties of satirist and commentator, yet contrived to retain in their work the distinctive quality of the artist. It is said of him that he was never more artistic than when he was under the most severe pressure, internal and external. Tradition has it that if you could get Duffy hopping mad to begin with, and then let the deadline creep upon him until the engraving room was howling bloody murder, his line grew swift and sure and his composition took on a balance and delicacy unsurpassed.

Which is probably fable; but it is fact that as a newspaper cartoonist he was not only the wielder of a mighty bludgeon, but also an artist of high attainments. His rating with Kirby as a three-time winner is no mistake.

18. If I Should Die Before I Wake

Jacob Burck, 1941

Jacob Burck, of the Chicago *Times,* Pulitzer Prize winner for 1941, published this cartoon June 2, 1940. At that moment the British were evacuating Dunkirk (May 26-June 4) and no one knew as yet how many men they had succeeded in getting off the beach; but everyone knew that disaster of the first magnitude had overtaken the allied democracies. Three weeks earlier Leopold of Belgium had damned himself to lasting infamy—and the loss of his crown—by surrendering 500,000 unwounded men, and France was to last just twenty days longer.

The condition of the average American on this date was one of stunned surprise. The amount of misinformation that had been fed to us by British and French propagandists during the preceding twelve months had laid us wide open to a terrific shock. The worst of it was that we were not deliberately deceived, or not to any great extent. Our European friends themselves believed the greater part of the nonsense with which they had been stuffing us with respect to the fine condition of the British and French armies—new evidence in support of Georges Clemenceau's sardonic remark, twenty years earlier, that war is too important to be left to the generals.

France was in fact excellently equipped to refight the war of 1914-18, and the British Navy was quite prepared to repeat the Battle of Jutland, this time with complete success. But when Hitler chose to fight with tanks and planes, instead of infantry and field artillery, the democracies were caught completely off balance. Nobody in the French high command, with the possible exception of the heretical De Gaulle, seems to have taken into consideration the probability that the Germans, instead of attacking the powerful Maginot Line, would simply walk around it. But they did, and their tanks raced down to Abbeville and the sea with ridiculous ease. In 1940 suspicion was rife that Hitler had bought Leopold, but it seems more likely that it wasn't necessary to buy him; the Germans simply scared him into a quivering mass of jelly. Such was the son of Albert the Great—Marcus Aurelius did no worse when he engendered the feeble Commodus.

It was not, therefore, merely the loss of territory and men and guns by the democracies that stupefied Americans, it was also their own loss of confidence in anything they were told by the British and French, and especially in the accuracy of their mental pictures of the Allies. The intelligence of France, the sturdiness of Britain, the heroism of Belgium, all had been proved illusions, all had been swept into limbo; and if these were false appearances, what could an American believe?

Well, there was the limitless woe that attends warfare. About that, there was no shadow of doubt, that was all too real. The armies could disintegrate and disappear, but the refugees were in plain sight. Churchill had not yet coined the phrase, "the red-hot rake of war," but its meaning was in our minds.

Accordingly sounds of confused lamentation arose all over the land, accompanied by the organization of countless committees with a wild wish at least to get the children out of it. It was more a sentimental gesture than a practical measure of assistance, although a few hundred children actually were brought to this country.

This is the mood that Burck's prize-winning cartoon reflects. Politically, it is neutral. The child in the ruins might be a child of any country, for the bombers were flying both ways. It is a protest against all war, not a denunciation of this particular crime, hence it must be relegated to the vapidly sentimental, a protest with no more edge to it than that of the sermon heard by President Coolidge, in which the parson announced that he was against sin.

But this is no proof at all that it misinterpreted the mood of the country. On the contrary, the most conspicuous characteristic of American thinking as the menace of the

"IF I SHOULD DIE BEFORE I WAKE . . ."

totalitarian dictators increased was its lack of edge. By so-called "neutrality acts" in 1934, 1935, 1936 and 1937 we deliberately bound our own hands; detesting crime, we forbade ourselves to make any distinction between criminals and honest men, which, in effect, ranged us on the side of the criminals.

Mussolini in Ethiopia, Franco in Spain, Hitler in Czechoslovakia and the Japanese militarists in Manchuria all profited greatly by our attitude. They plundered their victims at leisure while, like the Priest and the Levite in the parable of the Good Samaritan, we drew our garments about us and "passed by on the other side." True, by 1939 our policy had become so shockingly favorable to the international gangsters that we had reluctantly voted the "cash and carry" modification, allowing those nations that had plenty of money and plenty of ships to purchase supplies in our market. For the rest, we took it out in weeping scalding tears over the little girl praying by her bed. We wept for the child, but we had no intention of shooting down a bomber in her defense.

It was one of those periods in our history on which no American can look back with anything resembling satisfaction. Yet the basis of it was not either cowardice or greed, but lack of political maturity. Woodrow Wilson had brought us to the moral leadership of the world, but nobody had rendered us competent to play the role. We undertook to play that immensely complicated part by the rules of old-fashioned ward politics, which made disaster inevitable.

The first rule of cheap politics is to denounce your opponent as a scoundrel and a fool, from which it follows that whatever he did was both criminal and stupid. A really vigorous politician, however cynical he may have been to begin with, usually brings himself to believe his own nonsense. The attacks on Woodrow Wilson, at first intended merely to drive his party from power, were carried to such lengths that great numbers of people came actually to believe that the greatest American of the century was criminally insane, and that the war he won was robbery and murder on a cosmic scale. So we were swept into accepting the horrible heresy that there is no moral distinction between fighting for the right and fighting for the wrong. This is, of course, acceptance of the theory that no morality is binding upon a nation, a theory embraced by every bloodthirsty tyrant from Herod to Hitler.

There is no denying the fact that to stand up for what is obviously right is sometimes expensive. The catch in it is that not standing up for what is right is sometimes even more expensive. We didn't stop Mussolini in Ethiopia. We didn't stop Franco in Spain. We didn't stop Japan in Manchuria, or Hitler in Czechoslovakia, although we knew that every one of those raids was morally indefensible. But we did nothing because we weren't going to fight even a small war.

Today we know that each of these events was a step toward a big war, into which we were kicked by the Japanese. So we fought, after all, and it cost us three hundred thousand men and five hundred billion dollars. To have backed up the League of Nations, if necessary by fighting Mussolini in Ethiopia, certainly would have cost us no more and probably a great deal less; and it would have established us as a nation whose character commands respect.

To weep when a child is being abused is doubtless evidence of a good heart; but to knock the abuser into the gutter may be better evidence of good sense.

DIGRESSION ON THE MAN

Just before the outbreak of war in 1914 an immigrant brick-mason in Cleveland succeeded in bringing his wife and his nine-year-old son from Poland to this country. The boy went through high school and then into the Cleveland School of Art, where he developed the ambition to be a portrait painter, and with that in mind went to New York to study with Albert Sterner.

The boy was Jacob Burck. In New York he encountered a personality that exerted a more powerful influence on him than that of Sterner, a personality that has appeared again and again in these pages—Boardman Robinson. Burck himself says that he "sort of drifted" into newspaper cartooning. But when any young art student came under the influence of Robinson, and thereafter became a cartoonist, it is hardly to be described as a drift. It would be more accurate to say that he was swept into it.

Be that as it may, Burck, after doing some work for the *Masses,* then went to the St. Louis *Post-Dispatch,* and in 1938 to the Chicago *Times* where, three years later, he received the accolade of the Pulitzer Prize. When the Red Scare hit the country after the Second World War, Burck achieved an unpleasant notoriety because, in the depths of the Depression he had gone to Moscow on the promise of a job as a mural painter. The promise proved illusory, but Burck accepted a suggestion that he would get his claims advanced if he paid dues to the Communist party. He returned to this country disillusioned and strongly anti-Communist, but in 1955, under the law as it was then written, he was brought up for deportation. Nobody wanted to do it, because nobody believed he had been disloyal, but the law made no allowances. In the end, the Attorney General suspended the deportation order and the case was allowed to drop.

19. British Plane

Herbert L. Block, 1942

Exactly nine months before the "day of infamy," on March 7, 1941, the Newspaper Enterprise Association, a syndicate service, released a cartoon that brought into the list of Pulitzer Prize winners a name that was to become increasingly familiar through the next seventeen years. Formally, the name is Herbert Lawrence Block but, like Darling, known as Ding, it is more familiar in the telescoped form Herblock.

Twelve years later this cartoonist won again and when the two drawings are laid side by side it is difficult to attribute them to the same man, so marked is the difference in style. But one characteristic has not changed at all and it really establishes the identity of the work. It is what might be called the one-two punch. Herblock swings with both hands, and as a rule it is the delayed punch that is the haymaker.

Nine months before this cartoon was published France had gone down. Three months before it was published the desperate Battle of Britian, the war in the clouds, had roared to its terrific climax in the disastrous raid on London of December 29, 1940. This was the operation in which the neck of the British empire was to be wrung like that of a chicken; and already old Churchill, surveying the English landscape littered with the charred, bullet-riddled fragments of German aircraft, had made the definitive comment on the affair: "Some chicken! Some neck!"

Up to the time when this cartoon was drawn Americans had remained little more than stupefied spectators of the colossal drama. There had been no repetition of the loud and violent quarreling of 1916, when impressive numbers of Americans frankly adhered to the Kaiser. Nobody openly adhered to Hitler. Except for a small contingent of real Nazis who were singing pretty small in public, the isolationists were genuinely isolationist, not secretly pro-Hitler; their hope was not that Hitler might win, but that he would be defeated without our participation. By March, 1941, however, that hope was extinguished except in the breasts of those who resolutely shut their eyes to the facts.

That was the situation when Herblock, under the innocuous caption, "British Plane," pictured a German soldier in the street of a French city standing and gazing at the sky with impotent fury, his left hand clenched into a fist, his right on his useless pistol. It is a figure eloquent of baffled rage, the conqueror whose conquest was useless. That is Punch Number One. But huddled against the wall are three French civilians, poor, ragged, obviously in bad case—but they are secretly smiling. Punch Number Two—and this is the haymaker!

Herblock's admirers will strenuously contend that he has drawn dozens of better cartoons than this, and they are probably right. But the success of a Pulitzer Prize winner is measured, not by the technical excellence of the drawing, but by its impact upon the country at the time of its publication. In this respect Herblock reached a very high level here, and subsequent events proved that he was touched with prophetic insight. The future was the British plane in the sky, not with the momentarily victorious soldier on the ground.

It is arguable, of course, that the real success of this drawing is that it tapped the inexhaustible sentimentality of the American people, which is true. But it is a war cartoon, and what is war if not an explosion of the incurable sentimentality of the race? Hitler's Reich that would last for a thousand years certainly had little more relation to reality than Goldilocks' understanding with the Three Bears.

War is cruel, which is consistent with sentimentality. Mawkishness and heartlessness travel together without handicapping each other in the least. Elsie Dinsmore and Stalin professed equal concern for the welfare of humanity, probably with equal sincerity, and the hellish cruelty of Elsie to her dad yields

British Plane

to that of Stalin only on the point that the Russian had power of life and death.

In any event, sentimentality is a palpable force in the world, apparently irremovable. The wise realist is not he who deplores and despises existent forces, but the one with wit enough to apply them to some useful purpose. The sentimental appeal applied to the establishment of the Third Reich came near to destroying civilization, but the sentimental appeal of "blood, toil, tears and sweat" was a huge factor in its rescue.

The record of the *maquis* during the occupation of France is sufficient proof that Herblock was not lying. There was a secret smile on French faces during the darkest of those dark days. There were men in real life like the fictional Norwegian Mayor in *The Moon Is Down*. If Hitler had his dream of a Wagnerian opera that should last a thousand years, there was a counter-dream of a Millennial Dawn, and it was stronger than the spell of the Nibelungs. Such are the facts, and they render rather futile denunciations of sentimentality.

It is to be taken into consideration, of course, that the award was made about a year after publication of the cartoon, and by that time we were in the midst of the fight. But this is no sufficient proof that Herblock misstated the sentiment of the country as early as March, 1941. Resolution was hardening slowly, but it was hardening. The shock of the Japanese assault crystallized it very suddenly in the following December, but it is pretty certain that it would have crystallized anyhow. The fall of Moscow and Stalingrad would probably have done it had there been no Pearl Harbor. As it was, because Japan struck too soon, American food, gasoline and trucks poured into Russia in time to assist in stalling the German invasion before those cities fell. After that, the ruin of Hitlerism was certain.

This cartoon is a record of a certain moment in history that is not characteristically American, but that is visited on all democracies—the moment when individual opinions are slowly coalescing into something reasonably describable as the national purpose. It is a critical moment, more critical by far than Gettysburg, or Château-Thierry, or Midway, for it is the moment when democracies are most vulnerable. At such a moment a deadly thrust might not be parried, for while the necessity of fighting may be apparent to the well-informed, the ill-informed have not yet seen it, which means that there is as yet no effective will to fight.

It is a characteristic of democracies that baffles philosophers because philosophy has never yet formulated a convincing reason why any democracy has pulled out of its dream in time. Yet some have. Ours has, repeatedly. But exactly why and how irresolution is replaced by determination, nobody has ever explained. The early months of 1941 recall Mommsen's perplexed comment on the decision of the Romans in 270 B.C. to break out of Italy and challenge the power of Carthage across salt water in Sicily: "It was one of those moments when calculation fails, and men's faith in their own and their country's destiny alone gives them courage to grasp the hand which beckons to them out of the darkness of the future, and to follow it, they know not whither."

Or as certain of our own homespun philosophers phrase it: it's better to be born lucky than rich.

DIGRESSION ON THE MAN

Herbert Lawrence Block will appear again in these pages so perhaps it is enough to note here that this is not the Herblock known to the country in 1958.

This is not an intimation that the drawing presented here is a poor cartoon. It isn't. The idea is a powerful one, but in this drawing the cartoonist is evidently thinking more about his line than he was to think a dozen years later. Here is a man who knows his skill and is making a diligent and highly successful effort to employ that skill to drive home his idea.

When this same draftsman appears in the list of winners again it will be as a man who has forgotten he has any skill. He will have learned that if the idea is vital, and if he has conceived it clearly, the line will take care of itself. Skill will have been reduced below the threshold of conscious attention and thought will occupy not merely the center, but the whole of the stage.

This pair of cartoons holds a special interest in that it is the only exhibition that the series presents of the progression of a cartoonist from journeyman to master craftsman.

20. What a Place for a Waste Paper Salvage Campaign

Jay Norwood Darling, 1943

In 1943 J. N. Darling was awarded the Pulitzer Prize again—and for one of the feeblest cartoons he ever drew. Oh, there is humor in it, and a touch of satire, and the composition is mildly interesting. But this cartoon was published—in the New York *Herald-Tribune*—on September 13, 1942, in the midst of earth-shaking events, and it refers to waste paper!

In January of that year Corregidor had fallen. In February Singapore had fallen. On March 1, in the Battle of the Java Sea, the Navy had taken the worst punishment inflicted on it since Pearl Harbor. In May the drawn Battle of the Coral Sea at least saved Port Moresby. In June came Midway, turning point of the naval war, and in the same month, on the other side of the world, Rommel's triumphant sweep through Africa was checked at El Alamein. But also in that month Hitler launched his tremendous drive against Russia, and on the very day this cartoon was published German troops entered Stalingrad.

In August the Navy landed marines on Guadalcanal, lost the Battle of Savo Strait, and found that it had sent the marines into a trap. There ensued what was, considering the terrain, the climate, the enemy, and the logistic problem, probably the most utterly savage warfare in which American troops ever engaged. Army reinforcements reached the marines, but were themselves trapped. The Japanese landed a new army but it,

WHAT A PLACE FOR A WASTE PAPER SALVAGE
CAMPAIGN

in turn, was trapped. Not until November did the sea battle of Guadalcanal decide the question by finally closing the trap upon the enemy.

It was then solemnly adjudged that the best cartoon of a year filled with such events was one dealing with waste paper!

There were great cartoons published that year—Duffy's on Corregidor comes to mind at once—but most of them were of a kind to "fright the ladies," and the selection of any one would have given offense in some quarter at a moment when the clamor for unity was overwhelming.

With some plausibility it may be argued, too, that these powerful and to some people hateful pictures were not in the true line of political cartooning, whose armament consists of humor and satire. But when the heroic and the tragic are involved the satirist must walk warily, for a laugh at the wrong time is a deadly affront. The cartoonist is not a national hero, and in the presence of heroes it behooves him to sing low.

On the other hand war, from time immemorial, has never consisted exclusively of battle, murder and sudden death; it comprises, as well, a large element of idiocy. "Thy mandates make heroes assemble," declares the patriotic invocation to Columbia. True, beyond debate; but it is equally true that her mandates make asses assemble, and the people behind the lines are in more intimate contact with the asses than with the heroes.

Haste and some degree of confusion are inseparable from a great emergency, and haste and confusion inevitably result in the occasional appearance of incompetence in high places. The nation that wins a great war is not the one that has no incompetents in administrative positions, but the one that has a smaller percentage of them than the nation that loses. In 1942 our percentage of lunk-heads in key jobs was definitely smaller than that of our enemies. The event proved it; but in the midst of the war it was sometimes hard to believe.

In politics—in business, too, for that matter—there is no more definite proof of imbecility than the proliferation of useless reports. The useless report is the shield and buckler of official incompetence. The greater the stress the greater its value in that function and, therefore, the more astounding the rate of its multiplication.

In 1942 the country was fairly snowed under by such documents. The precipitation in 1958, in time of relative peace, is formidable, but it is light by comparison with wartime. When Ding's cartoon appeared people were suffering the worst affliction of the kind within the memory of living men, and that, not an incurable spirit of levity, accounts for the response to his drawing.

No good cartoon is altogether a joke. This one touched a genuine peril, lightly, but surely. There is not a general or an admiral alive who has not at one time or another looked darkly upon the possibility of defeat by typewriter rather than by the arms of the enemy. In fact, the first duty of a military staff is to prevent the loss of battles because the commander was too busy making out reports to give proper thought to the disposition of his forces.

But on the other hand, the best cartoon is always something of a joke. Ding's wild exaggeration of the situation in Washington gave people a chance to laugh at a moment when chances to laugh were tragically few; so, like the diamond, it gained enormously in value by its scarcity.

Sixteen years later it is the response to a joke that is the impressive and reassuring quality of this cartoon. It is evidence that at very nearly the worst moment of the war the American people retained the capacity to laugh at themselves. As regards the survival of the republic this has a significance that has been tremendously emphasized by events that have occurred since 1942, events of which Ding had no inkling.

A dozen years of cold war have pounded into us a new and disconcerting realization of the power of the psychological assault. There is no German Army on the march today, there is no Japanese Fleet upon the sea, yet millions of Americans feel more insecure than they felt in 1942. The phrase "brain-washing" has come into the vernacular and many there are who fear that it will overcome us where all armed forces failed.

But the psychologists have not been idle. They have subjected this process to intense and continuous scrutiny and have come up with some highly interesting information about it. They admit that any normal mind is vulnerable, given the right conditions. Whether it is a semi-literate hillbilly, or a Cardinal of the Roman Church, if the victim is subjected to sufficient pressure, physical and emotional, for a sufficiently long time, he will break, for the brain after all is a physical organ.

But some men break under very little pressure, while others resist for an astonishingly long time. The interesting discovery is that of the most resistant type. The man hardest to break down by "brain-washing" is not necessarily the most intellectual, the most learned, or the most devoted. It is the man who laughs.

In an individual it is certain that humor baffles Chinese or Russian torturers longer than any other psychological endowment. Does this apply equally to nations? Why not? Humorless Jurge Sewall could be driven into the madness of hanging old hags as witches, but not joke-loving Abraham Lincoln. The Germans who sang the "Hymn of Hate" in all seriousness could twenty years later be bamboozled by Hitler. But the British, who sang the "Hymn of Hate" satirically, could never be taken in by a Schicklgruber.

In the Valley of the Shadow in 1942 the American people could laugh at Ding's cartoon, although it stung one of their weak spots; and perhaps we were not only greater, but also safer then than later, when we shivered at McCarthy's ghost stories.

Digression on the Man

For many years Darling held a position among American cartoonists comparable in dignity to that of the dean of the diplomatic corps at Washington, and in personal esteem that of a beloved headmaster of a school. He taught a number of Pulitzer Prize winners and an undetermined number of other cartoonists; and he influenced practically every man in the business.

In cartooning he was the last great exponent of what is called the "cracker-barrel philosophy," that is, thinking influenced by a rural and small-town environment. To the rising generation much of Darling's work is probably incomprehensible because the barefoot boy is already a rarity, even in villages, and the farm population, strictly defined, is now reduced to about eleven per cent of the total.

Nevertheless, it was very fine work, narrow in outlook sometimes, but often penetrating human nature to a depth never reached by the more sophisticated observers whose youthful experience was confined to the city streets. Above all, it was psychologically solid, based on moral absolutes that no one thought of questioning, and steadied by a sense of humor that was a powerful solvent of all neuroses.

Darling's America is already old-fashioned and will soon be antique; but it touched greatness in its time.

21. But Where Is the Boat Going?

Clifford K. Berryman, 1944

Clifford K. Berryman, winner of the Pulitzer Prize in 1944, published his winning cartoon in the Washington *Evening Star* on August 28, 1943. In January of that year Tripoli fell to the British, in February Eisenhower was appointed to the supreme command in Africa, in May he received the surrender of the German African Army, in June he invaded Sicily, and July, Italy. In February the German Army trapped at Stalingrad surrendered, in August the new German offensive broke down, and by the end of the year the Russians were at the Polish border.

In the South Pacific furious naval-air battles followed one after another too fast for the American public to keep track of them. In March the Battle of the Bismarck Sea, in July the Battle of Kula Gulf, and in November the Battle of Empress Augusta Bay were successive blows that wrecked Japanese naval and air power in the south and left her land forces stranded to fall victim to MacArthur's steady northerly advance. Far to the north, in May, the Battle of the Komandorski Islands delivered the Aleutians, and in the center inexorable Nimitz, at Tarawa and Makin islands, began the advance that was to end in Tokyo Bay.

But the cartoon of 1943 that appealed to the judges dealt with no part of this tremendous drama, but with the squabbles taking place in Washington over our manpower mobilization. Berryman as a cartoonist harked back to the earlier style of Keppler and Gillam, with their careful attention to portraiture. McNutt, director of security, Hershey, director of the

But Where Is the Boat Going?

draft, Green, Murray and Lewis, labor leaders, are pictured recognizably as oarsmen of a boat, pulling against each other, while a conventional figure of Congress seeks to heave an anchor overside, despite McNutt's adjuration, "Remember, men, we're all in the same boat." The sardonic caption reads, "But where is the boat going?"

Of these, fifteen years later, only Lewis is remembered well enough for the casual observer to make an intelligent judgment of the caricature. But the helmsman is remembered. He is Franklin D. Roosevelt, and it is his face and figure that give the cartoon the savagery that lifts it out of the commonplace. It is all the more effective because of its careful avoidance of any gross distortion; its purpose is achieved by the insouciant air given to the man in a situation in which most people would say that insouciance was criminal.

To blast a victim not by any crude burlesque but merely by the position of an arm, by the angle of the jaw, by the set of the torso, is caricature indeed, but it cannot be denied that Berryman achieved it.

Nor is it to be denied that in so doing he touched an aspect of Roosevelt that has never been given the judicious examination it deserves. It has been remarked often enough, but almost always either with fury, or with adulation, almost never with plain curiosity. The man was incurably jaunty, and it can be argued plausibly that the angle of his cigarette holder maddened some people who had been able to endure all the legislation of the New Deal philosophically. In politics, four heavyweight championship bouts he won by a knockout, while one contender, Landon, never touched the canvas but sailed over the ropes to land among the pressmen's typewriters, the worst-beaten candidate since J. Q. Adams was given one electoral vote against James Monroe—and Adams wasn't even running. Taft in 1912 was not so badly whipped because he fought two heavyweights. But to the offense of winning monotonously Roosevelt added the further offense of winning with an air; and in the solemn purlieus of politics the Laughing Cavalier is regarded as a subversive character.

This was well known to every experienced cartoonist, of course, and they did what they could with it, although to little effect. As a rule, they overdid it. Roosevelt was one of the easiest of political figures to caricature admiringly, but one of the hardest to portray otherwise. Apparently he had something of the quality that David Low discovered in Lloyd George. In his autobiography Low says that time after time he used every trick of the trade he knew to make Lloyd George look sinister, and never succeeded. Countless times efforts were made to present Roosevelt in a repulsive light, but practically always the result was so gross and obvious a libel that it fell flat.

Berryman in this cartoon came about as near success as any man ever did. He had the wit to depict the man in a thoroughly characteristic attitude, with no more than trifling distortion of face or figure. He then built around him a situation in which the attitude was itself an indictment.

In so doing he represented with utmost fidelity the profound conviction of humorless characters, of whom there are myriads in the country. They were not all enemies of Roosevelt; on the contrary, the New Deal itself was loaded with solemn fellows whose lives were made miserable by their apprehension that the President would eventually laugh the whole program into ruin.

But while solemn friends worried and solemn enemies raved, the man with the charmed political life continued to step debonairly around a thousand pitfalls and gins, smiling through twelve of the most terrible years that even this terrible century has visited upon the republic.

One of Solomon's Proverbs says, "A merry heart doeth good like a medicine; but a broken spirit drieth the bones." Looking backward after fifteen years it seems plain enough that if the United States had gone through the worst of depressions into the most terrible of wars behind a broken-spirited leader, it would by now be little better than a valley of dry bones. Some people—indeed, many millions—felt it at the time, and to them the jaunty tilt of the long cigarette-holder was the most reassuring thing on the national scene. But there is no doubt that othes saw it as a bull sees a red rag. It was an incident in American history, and no comprehensive annalist should overlook it.

With the vastly efficient aid of hindsight one may easily work into this cartoon a parable that Berryman never thought of putting there, but that makes it more powerful than he dared hope. This is the lesson that in the utter confusion prevailing in the boat, the only man whom the event proved to be right was the only man who wasn't worried. This republic, like the rustic in the old story, has now lived a great many years and seen a great many troubles—the worst of which were those that never happened.

There is really nothing to be done about undue solemnity. Now, and presumably in all the years to come, it will continue to regard insouciance as a grave offense. So be it. But the solemn will certainly be more candid, and probably will suffer less, if they can make up their minds to admit that with regard to this crime, while they may condemn, history still retains the pardoning power.

DIGRESSION ON THE MAN

Clifford Kennedy Berryman was the senior member of the only father-and-son team that appears in the list of the prize-winners, and the relation was not entirely biological. The styles of the two men were so similar that readers of the Washington *Star* had to look at the signature to determine whether a specific drawing was by Clifford or his son James.

President Truman called the elder Berryman a great cartoonist "without malice." One may question that, for a cartoonist totally without malice is flavorless; but it is certainly true that Berryman was without viciousness. That is to say, he could and did expose his subject's faults ruthlessly, which comes within the definition of malice; but he never attributed to a man faults that were the figments of his own imagination, which is viciousness.

Berryman lived to the age of eighty and died in harness— he collapsed in the office of the *Star* on Armistice Day, 1949. Born in Kentucky, he never took a drawing lesson in his life, but few men have a career more satisfying from every point of view except, perhaps, that of the avaricious who count no man a success unless he has accumulated great wealth.

22. Fresh, spirited American troops, flushed with victory, are bringing in thousands of hungry, ragged, battle-weary prisoners

Bill Mauldin, 1945

William H. Mauldin took the Pulitzer Prize in 1945, although by no stretch of the definition could his work be called political cartooning. However, it was pictorial satire and it was too powerful to be ignored.

Ever since the cessation of hostilities Mauldin has fascinated analysts of all shades of opinion. They have reached the most contradictory conclusions about him and have offered impressive evidence in support of them all. Nobody denies that his war pictures were important, but there is little agreement on why they were important. Like all satire, his work is a protest, and like all good satire it is underlain by a profound moral earnestness. The immediate target of his protest is war.

Thus far the study of Mauldin's work presents no difficulty whatever, and thus far all critics are agreed. But beyond this point the material grows constantly more refractory and the divergences of the reputed authorities are so wide that one man's opinion is about as good as any other's. It is almost impossible to give a flat answer to any question about him. Does Mauldin hate war? Yes, but not frantically. He hates nothing frantically except staff officers whose speeding cars splash mud on plodding infantrymen. Does he love common soldiers? Yes, but not rapturously. All that enraptures him is the play of black against white so delicately balanced as to dissolve line, mass and perspective into emotion. Is Mauldin then a neuter, like the geometer's theoretical point, a *locus* without attributes? Perish the thought! The man is a bomb, charged with fury, grief, frustration, despair and every other explosive emotion.

To say that this picture, distributed to many newspapers in 1944 by the United Features Syndicate, is Mauldin's best would be to precipitate instant and clamorous warfare among his admirers. But it does possess one excellence in that it presents a plausible theory of his work. Read the words, "Fresh, spirited American troops, flushed with victory," and then gaze upon the figure representing them, a drooping expression of utter exhaustion, a total loss and no insurance! After the First World War another soldier, Laurence Stallings, in the same sardonic tone asked the American public, "What price glory?" That was in 1924. Exactly twenty years later Mauldin made answer: "A penny plain, and tuppence colored."

For present purposes, however, the cartoonist and his temperament may be disregarded. The significant thing is that he was popular, immensely popular, which means that his point of view coincided with that of millions of his fellow countrymen. There was dissent, of course. At the front there were martinets of the Prussian school who strongly favored hanging Mauldin; and at home there were addlepates who wished to see him impaled by the Dies Committee. If he escaped, it was because there were too many, both soldiers and civilians, who felt the truth of his presentation.

But this more than suggests the opening of a new chapter in national history. There is no question that Stallings' Captain Flagg, and Mauldin's Willie and Joe all fought well. The wreckage of six once great military powers—Austria-Hungary, Imperial Germany, Autocratic Turkey, Fascist Italy, Nazi Germany, and Japan—attests it. But the Americans fought with no thirst for glory, and military writers from Xenophon down have assumed that thirst for glory is an indispensable element of morale.

Mauldin's work has no bearing on strategy or tactics, but it administers a heavy jolt to traditional concepts of psychological warfare. Of course every experienced commander has always known that battle-hardened troops hold in lordly dis-

UP FRONT WITH MAULDIN

"Fresh, spirited American troops, flushed with victory, are bringing in thousands of hungry, ragged, battle weary prisoners." (News item.)

dain fanfares and flourishes and spectacular charges. Napoleon's Old Guard, Stonewall's Foot Cavalry, Sherman's Bummers, and Pershing's haughty division with the big, red One, required no drums and trumpets—only exact information as to what was to be done, whereupon they went and did it, disgustedly sometimes, but thoroughly.

But the military mind—perhaps one should say, rather, the general-staff mind, a special case of the military mind—seems to be unable to entertain the idea that there may be such a thing as a battle-hardened public that would act in much the same way. Mauldin did entertain the idea. At the start, he drew primarily for soldiers, but by the time the going got really rough he was drawing for the civilian public as well, and he fed them no sugary pap, no "fresh, spirited American troops flushed with victory." He gave them mud, rain, boredom, filth, cold, and above all fatigue, unimaginable, bone-crushing fatigue which, with hunger, consitutes the main fabric of war as the common soldier sees it.

The result? The civilian public laughed a little, wept a little, swore a little, and hardened and tempered its resolution with every drawing that was published. Neither up front nor behind the lines was pomp and circumstance, called by the Army spit-and-polish, at all essential to the creation and maintenance of high morale.

The popular success of Mauldin's work is fairly conclusive evidence that the lesson has come home to the people. When the Korean "police action" broke upon us, there was relatively little squalling of sentimentalists who hold that there can be no national misfortune unless some traitor has contrived it. A few cheap politicians tried to foment disaffection for their own profit, but with small success. Like veteran troops called up again, the nation settled to it with disgust, but without panic, and did what had to be done.

So now that the idea is common knowledge among the people, it is not unreasonable to hope that within a few years it may reach the people's leaders, for they are seldom more than a few years behind the masses. Then the excuse of maintaining morale will no longer be available to those who find the policy of keeping the people in the dark a most convenient means of covering up mistakes and incompetence. Perhaps we may eventually attain a concept of national security sounder than either the theory of the Maginot Line, or the theory of ambush based on the principle of lying in wait with unheard-of weapons. We may come to understand with our emotions, as well as with our reason, the true significance of the explanation why Sparta had no walls. She was safer without them, because in case of war every man knew exactly where was his place and what was his duty, and could be relied on to go there and do it.

This is, however, in the realm of speculation. Mauldin is no proof that it will come to pass, but he is a demonstration that it is possible. We have now to await the more remarkable demonstration that elected persons, commonly called popular leaders, are capable of seeing in time what is already as plain as day to the rank-and-file citizen.

Digression on the Man

In 1940 the Arizona National Guard, desperately trying to fill its ranks, was grabbing what it could get and giving physical examiners the raspberry. That is how it came to enlist a youth of eighteen who would have been rejected by any regular army medical officer. Five days later the Arizona Guard, as it stood, was taken into the Federal service.

That is why William H. Mauldin, physically unfit for active service, went through four years of war, was almost court-martialed by General Patton, caught a shell fragment at Salerno, which brought him the Purple Heart, became the idol, first of the army, then of the people at home, and at twenty-three appeared as the youngest of the Pulitzer Prize winners.

It was a process somewhat like a florist's hot-house forcing— the immediate results are splendid, but may not be particularly good for the plant. Mauldin has never achieved in time of peace the mordancy that made him by long odds the greatest cartoonist of the Second World War. His perception of the realities of politics has not approached the sharpness of his perception of the realities of war. If it had, there would be nobody in his class today.

Well, a man can't have everything, and surely it is enough for one man to have served his generation magnificently in one great crisis.

23. Time to Bridge That Gulch

Bruce Alexander Russell, 1946

There is grim irony in the fact that twelve years after its publication the prize-winner for 1946—it appeared in 1945—would be regarded as subversive propaganda in many quarters, perhaps including the Los Angeles *Times,* where it was published. Bruce Russell's drawing is an appeal for peace, and an appeal for peace was regarded as highly praiseworthy before the beginning of the cold war. But by 1957 a dozen years of bickering had made it politically dangerous for even as great a popular hero as President Eisenhower to speak of an understanding between the United States and Russia except in the most cautious terms.

In 1945 the Bear and the Eagle had just come to the end of a tremendous war in which they had fought on the same side. We had given lavish assistance in money and *matériel* to Russia; and in return Russia had destroyed a huge German Army that otherwise would have been hurled against us. To Russell, and to millions of other Americans, it seemed logical for the victorious super-powers to come to an amicable agreement regarding the reorganization and restoration of prostrate Europe. Any other course seemed at that time definitely irrational.

But another course was pursued, and we have much reason now to believe that it was irrational, not merely as the layman uses the word, but also in the medical sense. In his last days Joseph Stalin certainly cherished delusions of persecution, and it is quite possible that he had begun to lose his grip on

Time to Bridge That Gulch

reality by the time the war ended, or very shortly thereafter. His repudiation of the Yalta agreements was plainly not an act of balanced judgment, and his rejection of aid under the Marshall Plan was even further from reason.

But as far as the historical process is concerned, the fact that Stalin may have been losing his wits as early as 1947 is irrelevant. He was the dictator of Russia, and if every psychiatrist in America had known that he was definitely psychotic nothing could have been done about it. The suggestion is worth considering only because it does offer a credible explanation of a succession of events otherwise unaccountable on a rational basis.

The cold war may be said to have opened formally on November 3, 1946, when Foreign Minister Molotov delivered in the United Nations a speech that was a violent attack on the foreign policy of the United States; but before that it had become apparent that the Russian promises made at Yalta were not worth the paper they were written on. After the Molotov blast, the American riposte was the Truman Doctrine, announced in March, 1947; but it was quickly followed by the conciliatory gesture of the Marshall Plan. When Molotov denounced that as an imperialist plot for the enslavement of Europe, the cold war was really on and it continued without cessation for the next ten years.

Today it is impossible to recapture and difficult to comprehend the spirit of Russell's cartoon. The Bear is in a surly mood without doubt, but so is the Eagle, and there is no attempt to saddle the blame on one more than on the other. "Irresponsible statements" and "deepening suspicions" are mentioned, but it is impossible to say from which side they proceed. It must be remembered that up to this time Molotov had not brayed, and in this country there remained a widespread admiration of the courage and strength that Russia had displayed in the war.

Even then, except in a small group of fanatics, there was no liking in this country for the Communist form of government. But, except in another small group of fanatics, there was no disposition here to deny the Russian people's right to live under any form of government they chose to tolerate. Most intelligent Americans believed that in the undeveloped resources of Russia and the still unreleased energies of her people there were immeasurable possibilities for the advancement of civilization. As far as that goes, intelligent Americans still believe it; what they have lost is their optimistic faith that the work could be done quickly and with relative ease.

We have learned through the cold war that whether or not Stalin was already failing mentally in 1947, the totalitarian system leaves the whole world vulnerable to the intellectual deterioration of one man. For the response to unreason is invariably unreasonable. As Falstaff was not only witty himself but also the cause that wit was in other men, so the years have proved that madness in Moscow is the cause that insanity is in Washington. Twelve years after the end of the Second World War one-half of the revenues of the government, being one-tenth of our total national production, must go down the drain to keep millions of armed men on watch because we have never been able to reach an understanding with Russia. Russell's gulch has widened into a chasm that threatens to swallow the world.

As regards prophetic insight, this cartoon is unquestionably one of the world's worst; and it is the great tragedy of our times that this is true. The caption was accurate; it was the time to bridge that gulch. But the time was allowed to pass, and the opportunity has not returned since. Yet the assumption that it was possible even then to bridge it rested on the further assumption that there were on both sides men of great skill and great tenacity who were determined to bridge it. Enough such men never appeared.

We have the rather cold comfort of knowing that on our part some effort was made and continued to be made. No rational man can deny the diligence and energy of Marshall, Acheson and Dulles, and most of us believe that a comparable effort on the other side could have done the work. But we have no ground for complacence. If Stalin grew more and more unbalanced as the years passed, so did no small number of Americans, including some of the loudest-mouthed in the country. Vishinsky and Molotov perhaps remain unrivaled masters of vituperation, but at that they did not greatly surpass some Americans. Our advantage is that none of our worst held the office of Secretary of State, while Molotov was the Russian Foreign Minister.

The sombre truth is that while we have more or less successfully contained Communism, we have not contained the deterioration in rational thinking that has been spreading from Moscow until it now infects the whole diplomatic world. Stalin's delusion of persecution may fairly be described as epidemic among heads of states today. They shudder at every creak upon the stairs; they start at every flutter of the window curtains; their voices have grown steadily more querulous and high-pitched until the normal tone of diplomatic conversation has risen into a shriek.

Our foreign service has never been permitted to go in for gaudy vesture, but certain long-established conventions were observed. As late as 1945 the approved apparel of an American ambassador include a silk hat, cutaway coat and striped trousers, raiment supposed to be consonant with the dignity of his discourse. Some still adhere to the clothes, but the consonance no longer exists; were he to dress the part today, the diplomat would dance into the audience-chamber to the rhythm of tom-toms, bedizened with war-paint, belted with knuckle-bones, and whirling a watchman's rattle in each hand.

Irrational it certainly is; but "so runs the world away."

DIGRESSION ON THE MAN

Bruce Alexander Russell, another product of the Far West, is also another graduate from commercial art to cartooning. Born in Los Angeles in 1903, he put in seven years as a staff artist for the *Times,* of that city, before becoming political cartoonist. But his record is unusual in that he had served a hitch as cartoonist before he undertook commercial work. He was with the *Herald* in that capacity for a year before joining the *Times.*

His education he obtained in the Los Angeles public school system and the University of California at Los Angeles, but as a craftsman he was largely self-taught. His prize-winning cartoon, however, shows a careful attention to detail that one associates with rigid academic training; perhaps it is a legacy from the days when his work had to satisfy advertisers who were more interested in accuracy than in ideas.

Russell did a comic strip called Rollo Rollingstone for the Associated Press for some years, but soon discovered that his real talent was for political comment rather than fantasy.

24. Still Racing His Shadow

Vaughn Shoemaker, 1947

The winning cartoon of 1947—drawn by Vaughan Shoemaker, of the Chicago *Daily News*—might as easily have been the winner in 1957, or for that matter, in 1837, and it is all too likely that it will still be highly appropriate fifty years hence.

It is an optical illusion in a double sense, designedly and undesignedly. A race against one's shadow is an illusion, as Shoemaker knew when he made the cartoon; what he didn't know, and could hardly guess, was that his racer would be regarded, ten years later, as a starting-post, not moving at all. In 1957 the ultimate authority, the *Statistical Abstract of the United States,* was presenting the cost-of-living index as ranging about 120, with the explanatory note "1947-49 = 100;" and it continued to rise. That is to say, Shoemaker's furious runner is today the static figure from which we measure the extent of our woe.

Shoemaker's cartoon is timeless in that it presents one of those truths that all men know and no man really believes, except in moments of extreme melancholy. It is the truth that all money is to some extent like the magician's coins in the *Arabian Nights.* They were so new and shiny and beautifully minted that the merchant who received them separated them from the rest of his money and put them in a drawer apart; but some time later, when he took them out, they had turned into withered leaves.

The United States mint was established in 1792, and its product has been remorselessly depreciating in value ever since

Still Racing His Shadow

—not steadily, for it has had spurts when it has risen above last year's value, and even the value of five years before. But the dollar has never risen to where it was twenty-five or fifty years earlier, and the strong presumption is that it never will.

This fact is known to every first-year student of economics, but it is not really believed by anyone, because it is inadmissible in the practical conduct of business, which is inevitably based on accepted fiction. A scrap of paper, printed in black on one side and in green on the other, is not intrinsically worth a shirt priced at five dollars, but you have no difficulty in obtaining the shirt by presenting the scrap. The fiction agreed upon permits the transaction of business.

What is equally true, but not so readily admitted, is that the stamped disks of gold that formerly passed as money also decreased in value with the passage of time, not merely by the gradual rubbing away of the metal, but also by a slow but incessant reduction in the value of the metal. If the law would permit you to have a coin of 129 grains it would now buy a steak in a first-class restaurant; but in the reign of Elizabeth the Great it would have bought a steer, and in the time of Julius Caesar it would have bought a butcher, although the weight of the gold had remained constant.

This comes into head-on collision with the vain, but ineradicable, human yearning for stability; therefore it is denied and its assertion is hotly resented. Religion perhaps excepted, nothing in human history has been more productive of turmoil, revolt and revolution than the introduction of bad money into any commercial society. Counterfeiting, clipping and sweating have always been regarded as heinous offenses, in most countries closely allied to high treason, with penalties ranging up to life imprisonment and death. Kings and emperors have lost their thrones and some their heads because they were suspected of debasing the coinage.

So the thought that all money is bad money is flatly intolerable and is not accepted; thus when a particular coinage, as for instance the dollar, is obviously deteriorating, we usually choose to attribute the debasement to the machinations of some villain and demand his head. If there is no individual scoundrel conveniently at hand, we pick upon some class— frenzied financiers, or greedy monopolists, or power-mad labor leaders; and as a rule there is just barely enough truth in these charges to make them stick.

Note Shoemaker's confidence that "new wage demands" cast the shadow that the workman is racing. Ten years later, when the cost of living was inflated twenty per cent beyond its height in 1947, it was an article of faith with many business leaders that extravagant overpayment of labor was the cause of the inflation. Labor leaders were equally certain that extravagant overpayment of stockholders in profits and dividends was responsible. It is a moral certainty that both were right, in a measure. But the real villain of the piece was probably neither, but simply the failure of all hands, including not only capital and labor, but the learned doctors of economics as well, to bring our understanding of the theory of distribution abreast of our understanding of the theory of production.

Some progress unquestionably has been made. Thirty-five years ago when the Boston merchant, Edward A. Filene, was proclaiming the doctrine that mass production is properly production of masses of customers, not masses of goods, he was a voice crying in the wilderness and half the business world thought he ought to be locked up for his own good. But the doctrine is a commonplace today. Not money but consumer demand makes the mare go; and if there is no money to make consumer demand effective, it must be created, by credit, or by subsidy, or by any other device that will get it into consumers' hands.

The catch is that inflation follows. That is the bug that we have never yet worked out of the economic machine. But it is definitely an advance to have discovered that a bug in the design is the trouble, not some saboteur deliberately plotting to stall the works. The more time we waste looking for a saboteur who isn't there, the longer it will be before we get at the real cause of the trouble.

It will be a long time at best, for an understanding of the relativity of economic "law" will take a long time to percolate into a sufficient number of minds. That is why it is a safe prediction that Shoemaker's cartoon will still be apt when today's small boys have grown long gray beards. But perhaps it is not too much to hope that the sound and fury may be somewhat reduced, even though the dispute goes on.

In fact, it has already lessened appreciably, as every senior citizen with a long memory knows. Today the *Wall Street Journal* can print essays on the most abstruse kinds of monetary theory without raising more than a slight suspicion that the staff has either sold out to the Bolsheviki, or fallen victim to dementia, senile or praecox. There was a time by no means as long ago as the span of a single life when to discuss Keynesian economics in the presence of a banker with hypertension was, if not attempted homicide, at least criminal negligence; while to attempt a fair assessment of the value of management at a union meeting was an invitation to mayhem.

Small gains, no doubt, but any gain at all furnishes ground for speculation that may range far and wide. In the world that Einstein has opened nothing is certain, not even that Shoemaker's desperate racer will never outrun his shadow.

DIGRESSION ON THE MAN

Vaughan Shoemaker's second Pulitzer Prize—his oak-leaf cluster, so to speak—is one winning cartoon that may fairly be classed with the man's best work, at least from the technical stand-point.

As an action picture, this one is undeniably there with the goods. The double impression of speed and strain in his running figure is immense. But to that the artist has contrived to add an element that gives the drawing a value outside the field of esthetics, and it is this that makes it a cartoon, rather than merely an illustration.

One feels that this is not merely a workman, but a good workman—no shiftless feather-bedder, but a craftsman in the best sense. If he hung a door it would swing true, if he soldered a joint it would be watertight, if he fixed a clock it would keep time. Such a man ought not to be driven to desperation by the effort to pay his grocer's bills. In the very act of criticizing, Shoemaker traps us into sympathy for the object of his criticism.

This, you may object, is not art, it is philosophy. It may be so; but the journalist is certainly part philosopher and the true cartoonist is a journalist. Art, philosophy, or what not, this element is indubitably good cartooning.

25. Peace Today

Reuben L. Goldberg, 1948

R euben L. Goldberg has always been a social rather than a political satirist, his chosen target being the American adoration of gadgets. In his youth Goldberg was educated as an engineer and later he developed as his characteristic technique a satire on mechanical drawing, which his rich imagination carried to an extravagance never reached by anyone else.

But on August 6, 1945, Goldberg's special field suddenly coincided with the field of international politics, for on that day, over the city of Hiroshima, a great naval base in Japan, Americans demonstrated the gadget to end all gadgets, and possibly to end all mankind, as well. The atomic bomb was an extravagance at which the imagination even of a Goldberg boggled.

The full significance of the thing was revealed only by degrees (it has not been clearly revealed yet) and it was not until 1947 that Goldberg made his comment on it in a cartoon published in the New York *Sun*. But when he did comment he won the Pulitzer Prize.

The first impression made by the picture called "Peace Today" is of its extraordinary simplicity—for Goldberg. But it is natural enough, when one stops to think. Here was a subject beyond the power of the champion exaggerator to exaggerate; so, being a resourceful satirist, he took the other tack and made it fantastically simple—a shell delicately balanced on the verge of an abyss, with a house perched on the shell and a family serenely enjoying life at a crazy angle.

But the craziest angle of all was not given it by Goldberg, but by old Father Time. This was the world of 1947, without doubt, and a strange one it was; but eleven years have passed and it is now the world of 1958, which is twice as strange. Knowing our peril, in more than a decade we have done nothing effective toward reducing it!

If anyone could tell us plainly why this is so, he would speak with the tongue of men and of angels, but part of the answer undoubtedly is in the side of American character that Goldberg had been needling for many years before 1947, the adoration of the gadget. Myriads of us still cling to a childlike faith in our ability to invent another gadget that will preserve us from the deadly one that exploded in 1945. Yet how could there be plainer proof than Hiroshima that the cult of gadgetry, carried to its logical extreme, ends in destruction? Must nine-tenths of us be vaporized to convince the surviving tenth? And suppose that by some very slight miscalculation the operation should be ten-tenths effective—what then?

In his grisly novel, *On the Beach,* Nevil Shute contemplates this possibility. This book-length whimper asserts that the remnant would continue to act just as idiotically as before until the last surviving specimen of *Homo sapiens* committed suicide to escape dying agonizingly in the radioactive air. This is tantamount to a finding that the species is a worse failure, biologically, than pterodactyl or dinosaur, since *homo* is destined to exterminate not only himself, but all other forms of life.

The Shute hypothesis may be a sort of literary Rube Goldberg machine, but if it is rejected, with what is it to be replaced? In formal logic, nothing. But formal logic is not the only realm invaded and, in a measure, dominated by the human mind. There is also the realm of fantasy, and if it includes the dismal extravagances of Shute, the fatalist, it also includes the diverting extravagances of Goldberg, the humorist. They are antithetical, yet only a hairline separates them, and both enter into the composition of the creature that reminded Falstaff of a forked radish.

About the time of the First World War the same New York *Sun* that published this cartoon carried a metrical demonstration of the tiny divergence that makes all the difference.

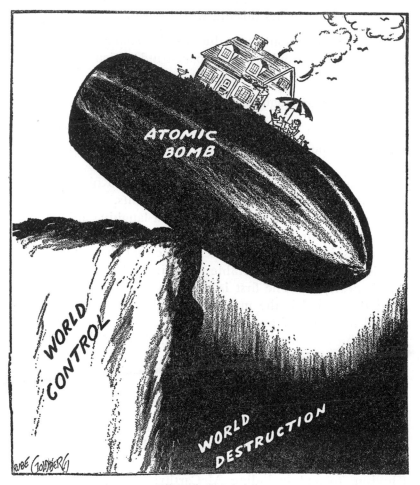

PEACE TODAY

A poetaster complained of the intelligent compositor—doubtless apocryphal—who had attributed to him the "ultra-Prussian" sentiment,

> Manslaughter is the wholesome thing
> That makes this old world sweet.

This melancholy result was due to the compositor's having dropped an apostrophe and a space-band which, if properly inserted, would have made the first line,

> Man's laughter is the wholesome thing,

and the versifier would have been extracted from the school of Diogenes the Cynic, and placed in that of Aristophanes, the comedian.

Into our litany of adoration of the gadget Rube Goldberg sticks the punctuation that Nevil Shute omits. Man, after all, is not nearly so much a logical as he is a laughing animal. Dr. William Sargant, that assiduous student of the process of "brain-washing," has produced evidence that there is one man who is completely invulnerable to brain-washing, and another who is nearly so. The first is the man who is crazy to begin with; the second is the man who laughs. An insane man is beyond the reach of psychological suggestion, a man endowed with a sense of humor almost beyond it. The possible inference that the humorist is half crazy is ignored in this place as not pertinent to the argument.

The historical record offers considerable support to the theory that the manias to which the American people fall victim from time to time are seldom eliminated by logical argument, but are nearly always blasted by laughter. From Know-Nothingism through Anti-Masonry, Prohibition and Ku Kluxism, to and including McCarthyism, the wrath of the righteous availed little, but the gibes of the comedians were ruinous. As regards any widespread popular movement, when a sufficient number of Americans decide that the whole business is silly, that's that.

Of course, historical evidence is never conclusive because there is always a first time. Some super-Huey Long may yet arise to take us down the same road along which Hitler led the Germans. But it is not inevitable, and nothing is more absurd than to cherish the delusion that every wart must be an incipient cancer.

In Goldberg's cartoon the attitude of the family under the beach umbrella is irresistibly comic—bitterly so, but comic nevertheless. Perhaps before it is too late the conviction will come home to the American people that this perpetual teetering on the brink of destruction is not only terrifying, but utterly ridiculous, as well; and if that conviction arrives, they will demand of their leaders effective action toward reducing the peril. Then if they don't get it, they will boot out of office leadership that can only gabble and wring its hands, replacing it with leaders having wit enough to think of something new and nerve enough to do it.

But that time has not come yet. Goldberg's bomb, balancing on the edge of the cliff, is as appropriate a description of the situation today as it was eleven years ago. To this day our answer to the peril is not an improvement in international relations, but more bombers, newer weapons, fancier "civil defense"—palliatives, not cures. In this respect there has been no change in more than a decade, although most men agree that time is running out.

The fact that with danger approaching in the night the dog did nothing Sherlock Holmes considered more remarkable than anything that did happen.

DIGRESSION ON THE MAN

Reuben Lucius Goldberg obviously doesn't belong in this gallery, but what of that? He doesn't belong in any other gallery, either, except in the vast and fascinating gallery of odd characters in American history. It isn't that there is anything especially startling in the man's personality. Born in San Francisco in 1883, he took a Bachelor of Science degree at the University of California, married, begot two sons and as husband and father lived a decorously uneventful life.

But professionally he was born of an earthquake and never managed to get the world rightside-up again. He was a sewer engineer in 1906 when San Francisco slid and all engineering was reduced to utter futility. Goldberg emerged from the rubble no longer an engineer, but an illustrator, not of the day's events, but of phenomena beyond space and time, the phantasmagoria of people from under whose feet the earth has fled.

On the old New York *Mail*—long since vanished—he became immensely popular, and later, on the *American,* became a national institution. But he has been political only in rare and aberrant moments. Goldberg is the satirist not of fads and fancies but of rationality; and in that capacity he has had countless imitators but never a serious rival.

But he is not a political cartoonist, and he became a Pulitzer Prize winner only because he touched a spot where so-called rationality had become absurd.

26. Who, Me?

Lute Pease, 1949

John Llewellyn Lewis was without doubt one of God's greatest gifts to American cartoonists in the twentieth century. His physical appearance made him easy to caricature and his salient personality constantly brought him into situations lending themselves to satire. It is not that Mr. Lewis was ever a comic character, but that he was masterful, and a truly masterful man is always running into situations in which there is an element of comedy.

It was with his treatment of such a situation that Lute Pease, of the Newark *Evening News,* won the Pulitzer Prize in 1949. In the previous year the coal miners, whom Mr. Lewis had led through many turbulent years, threatened a nation-wide strike, and to prevent it the Truman administration invoked the Taft Hartley law, which Mr. Truman had vetoed two years earlier only to have it passed over his veto. The excuse was that a coal strike was so grave a threat to the national economy as to justify resort to a law that the President questioned.

Lewis denied that the strike was a threat to the nation and this is the subject of the cartoon. It is one of Pease's most successful, both for the economy of means and the excellence of the caricature, which combine to produce an instantaneous effect, needing no explanation. A cartoon that can be put over with the two words, "Who, Me?" is incontestably a good cartoon.

Yet it would have been relatively a failure without the distinctive place that the chief figure occupied in American life at the time—and since, for that matter. John L. Lewis became a great labor leader through a combination of qualities rare in any kind of man but that, when present, would make one distinguished in any walk of life. The combination includes energy, courage, prudence, and a flair for the dramatic. This last quality was tremendously important because through it Lewis was frequently able to give what was in fact an exceedingly cautious move the appearance of wild recklessness. He always knew when he was beaten, and as a rule he knew it before the opposition did, and so was usually able to withdraw his forces still intact. This has enabled him to survive more defeats than any other labor leader in his class.

It also made him the darling of the reporters, for there was always a story in Lewis. It is easy to believe that he could make top-of-the-column, page one, by reciting the multiplication table, and not once but repeatedly he did paraphrase passages from *The Wealth of Nations* and make them sensational.

He owed his success in this respect chiefly to a style that was unique. Son of a poor miner, he went into the mines as a boy, and his formal schooling was of the slightest; but somehow he acquired a thorough knowledge of the English Bible, King James version, the most sonorous English ever written; and he added to that a notable familiarity with the works of William Shakespeare. Perhaps from his Welsh ancestors, musical people, he inherited a fine appreciation of the rhythms of the spoken language. The sum of all this was little short of wizardry. John L. Lewis could, as the saying goes, talk a bird off the bough, an old man from the chimney-corner, the ears off a brass monkey.

It is true that this was a tricky weapon that sometimes backfired with devastating effect. Once, on a subject now forgotten, Lewis came into violent collision with John Nance Garner, then Vice President of the United States, and vented his exasperation by calling Garner "a poker-playing, whisky-drinking, evil old man." He produced an effect, all right, but not the one intended. From Sandy Hook to the Golden Gate the roars of laughter were stupendous, for in a single phrase Lewis had touched the risibilities of the country three times.

In the first place, while there were plenty who regarded

Who, Me?

Cactus Jack Garner as archaic, nobody believed he was evil; yet many who had felt the edge of his sharp tongue giggled when he got his comeuppance, for they felt that Jack had long been asking for it. Joke Number One.

In the second place, the spectacle of the leader of the coal miners, themselves no lily-fingered sissies, professing to be shocked by the Texan's partiality for a glass and a friendly game of stud was uproariously comic, a magnificent example of Satan rebuking sin. Joke Number Two.

Finally, the sheer lilt of the words, "poker-playing, whisky-drinking, evil old man," had a jolly swing that was bound to provoke a chuckle, no matter who uttered them. Number Three. The thing was irresistible, and when it appeared that both Garner and Lewis were taken aback by its reception it grew funnier than ever. Like many another, Lewis suffered the mishap of becoming unforgettable by miscalculation.

However, that was a trifling episode in a long and resounding career. John L. Lewis managed to get himself as violently hated as any man in America, but his triumph was that four times out of five he was hated by the right people. He in turn developed tremendous hatreds, a memorable one for Franklin D. Roosevelt, which was an error. However, it was probably inevitable, for in Roosevelt, Lewis encountered the only man in the country who could surpass him in that peculiar combination of courage and wariness that was much of Lewis' own strength.

His supreme achievement, of course, was his realization that the industrial union is the answer to the vertical corporation and his effectiveness is doing something about it. To form the Congress of Industrial Organizations he had to split the American labor movement and it is characteristic that he did not hesitate to split it, yet did so with a prudence that did not destroy the movement. Later, he split the CIO, to what ultimate effect is not yet clear, although it seems to have forced the reunion of AFL and CIO.

Yet when all is said and done, the factor that has made Lewis the delight of Pease and every other cartoonist is none of his extraordinary qualities, but a very ordinary one indeed, to wit, common decency. John L. Lewis may be the terror of the age, but he is no racketeer. He keeps his hands off the union funds, he maintains no high-priced brothels, he bribes no police chiefs, he doesn't present motor cars and country estates to crooked politicians. By forcing the wages of coal miners up, they say he has robbed United States Steel, and the power companies, and the railroads, in a high, wide and handsome manner; but he never sent a goon squad to put the bite on some wretched Chinese laundryman, or poor Negro pants-presser. This gives all decent men a measure of respect for him, a respect that was never produced by his rolling thunder.

Look again at Pease's cartoon. There is no exculpation in it. That devilish small boy is getting what was coming to him, and richly he deserves it; but by no stretch of the imagination can one see any real vice in the picture. The crime had its root not in viciousness, but in lack of judgment; and one can hardly get rid of a suspicion that maybe smashing the window was the logical thing to do.

There is the summation of John L. Lewis. If one must call him merely one of the great labor leaders, not flatly the greatest, the reason is that lack of balanced judgment. One suspects that if in his early years he had mastered his Montaigne as thoroughly as he did his Shakespeare, the word for him might have been "greatest" without modification.

DIGRESSION ON THE MAN

Lucius Curtis Pease is the inspiration of the gaffers, for he won the Pulitzer Prize five weeks after his eightieth birthday— its oldest recipient. Moreover, at that time he was turning his attention to painting in oil with an especial liking for seascapes. He confided to reporters that he hoped to be well-known by the time he was ninety.

His was not only the longest, but the most variegated career among the prize-winners. Born in Nevada, in 1869, he was orphaned at the age of five and was brought up by his Pease grandfather in Vermont. He was educated at Franklin Academy, in Malone, N.Y., where his maternal grandfather had been a judge. He wished to study art, but financial consideration forbade, so he went to California and from there to the Klondike in the gold rush of 1897-8. But he found little gold, became a hotel manager, and eventually United States Resident Commissioner in Nome. Back in Portland he became a magazine editor and published the early work of Jack London. But on account of his wife's health he eventually returned to the East, free-lanced for a year, and in 1914 became cartoonist for the Newark *Evening News*. It was in the thirty-sixth year of his service on that paper that he won the award.

Well, all one can say, after noting the vigor, the humor and the punch in this cartoon, is, "Eighty, eh? He certainly doesn't look it!"

27. All Set for a Super-Secret Session in Washington

James T. Berryman, 1950

J ames T. Berryman's winning cartoon in 1950—published the year before in the Washington *Evening Star*—is ostensibly a sardonic comment on Washington's appetite for publicity. The setting for "a super-secret session" includes every instrumentality of publicity—radio, television, Klieg lights, movie cameras, telephones and a typewriter-equipped press table. The stateliness of the chairs behind the conference table gives a touch of burlesque dignity to the composition, and the absurdity of the identification letters on the mikes, "WAHU," "WUWU," and "WHIM" is the newspaper man's crack at his rival, the radio newscaster.

It is an entertaining piece, good-humored, yet spiced with enough malice to save it from being a mere honey-bun, and it is certainly one hundred per cent American—a statement with which some who agree will agree ruefully. For there are those who find in the Americanism of the American governmen its fatal defect.

It is a reasonable assumption that Berryman's cartoon was a hit in 1949 because although it spoke jestingly, it spoke truthfully of an American Dilemma as perplexing as the one about which Myrdal wrote two volumes. If we assume that the American government exists—at times a doubtful proposition— we face at once the difficulty that it cannot be American without what Woodrow Wilson called "pitiless publicity" and it cannot be government with utterly pitiless publicity.

This establishes a condition of endless warfare between the media of publicity and the agencies of government. Each in going about its lawful occasions is bound to come into frequent and sometimes violent collision with the other, and the servants of each, the newsmen and the politicians, like the herdsmen of Lot and the herdsmen of Abram, live in incessant strife. Nor is there any possibility of a Thirty-Eighth Parallel defining and separating their spheres of influence, for they are mutually dependent. The politician cannot survive without publicity, nor the reporter without copy. A symbiosis associates them like that of the termite and the parasite that enables him to digest wood; and to break the connection would mean extinction for both.

This uneasy relation is one of alternate loving and loathing. There is no crime in Newgate Calendar of which either will not readily and fervently accuse the other; and there is no service, not excluding laborious and dangerous service, that either will not render the other under appropriate circumstances.

The state of warfare is too obvious to be overlooked by the most careless observer; what is overlooked, sometimes by otherwise competent students of public affairs is that, to borrow a famous phrase, "we planned it that way." The Constitutional provision that Congress shall make no law abridging freedom of speech or of the press is a guarantee of strife.

Furthermore, it is consonant with the rest of the structure of government. *The Federalist: Number Ten* is usually construed as Madison's effort to reassure the people as to the stability of the new republic, which, of course, it is. But we examine less carefully the significance of his theory of stability, which is the theory of "checks and balances," the stability that is in fact the resultant of equal and opposing forces.

Everyone knows that the Constitution is a carefully worked-out formula regulating checks and balances within the fabric of government; but Madison, in Paper Number Ten, extrapolated the calculation to cover the whole social structure that includes the fabric of government. "Great Little Jemmy" was no soothsayer, so of course he never imagined the enormous complexity of the social structure that exists today; but he and his colleagues in the Constitutional Convention had a mirac-

ALL SET FOR A SUPER-SECRET SESSION IN WASHINGTON

ulous grasp of fundamental principles, and they apply whether one is building a chicken-coop or a skyscraper. One of those principles is the balancing of stresses.

Berryman, as a journalist, was fighting on his own side in this cartoon, but for all that the drawing reveals to a thoughtful examiner something of the situation of the other side. In this case the implication is that the instruments of publicity were placed there by conferees whose professed desire for secrecy was hypocritical, which is the case often enough. On the other hand, it is a reminder that public life is in fact public. The cameras are there, whether they are desired or not, and anyone who has sat in the glare of the Kleig lights knows that the most difficult of all poses to assume under them is one of relaxation.

As silicosis is the logical fate of the gold miner, and the bends that of the diver, so the politician may expect to end as a stuffed shirt. It is his occupational disease, and the most elaborate protective measures are no sure defense against it. The one injection that offers practically perfect immunity is humor; but from the politician's standpoint that remedy is worse than the disease, because too stiff a dose will result in paralysis of the political functions.

The classical example is the Hon. James Proctor Knott, of Kentucky, a man whose abilities should have carried him at least as far as the Cabinet, but who was wrecked by one speech in the House of Representatives. It was the famous oration on Duluth, which he extolled as "zenith city of the unsalted seas," and it was a masterpiece of satire against a pork-barrel bill. It killed the bill, but it also killed Knott, because thereafter whenever he rose to his feet the House began to laugh before he had said a word. As Keith Preston put it in his remark on Whistler:

> And, like the tail that wagged the dog,
> The smart tale dogs the wag.

Perhaps another example is the Hon. Adlai Stevenson, whose campaign for the Presidency in 1952 was the most brilliant on record: but when he ran again in 1956 the country expected him to surpass his first effort, and when he failed to do so he got fewer votes than he had in 1952.

In any event, Berryman's cartoon is food for thought. Apply

it to yourself. Fix your attention on those chairs. Imagine yourself, being Joe Doakes, no genius but a decent citizen making
a fair living and getting along pretty well with the neighbors,
occupying one of those seats of the mighty and facing that
battery of machinery hooked, as you are well aware, to all
national radio and TV networks. How long would you
remain Joe Doakes? Not for ten seconds. After that, you would
be the Hon. Joseph Preposterous Doakes, member of the Congress of the United States representing the great state of Win-
nemac, Gateway to the Golden West and Priceless Pearl of
God's Own Country. And, unless protected by some special
dispensation of Divine Providence, you would begin to look
like a jackass before the chairman's gavel had rapped twice.

Don't you know it? If you do, think how remarkable it is
that some members of Congress—hardly a majority, but still
an impressive number—manage to remain relatively human in
spite of the publicity that attends their official positions.

"The fierce white light that beats upon a throne" is a good
phrase. It's fierce, all right—both in itself and in what, unhappily, it reveals, as, for example, what Senator Joseph Mc-
Carthy really looked like.

DIGRESSION ON THE MAN

James T. Berryman, junior member of the only father-and-son
team in the list of prize-winners—his father won in 1944—is so
perfectly "old" American that it is doubtful that he is American
at all in the modern sense. He was born in Washington, D.C.,
which absolves him of any state or regional allegiance. His
forebears fought in the Revolution, and on both sides in the
Civil War; and he and his father have been vigorous opponents
of any change in the political and social systems of the country,
which made them highly critical of the Roosevelt and Truman
regimes.

But both father and son have been for many years the delight of the "cave-dwellers" that is, the relatively small permanent population of Washington, those persons who are not
engaged in politics and therefore do not change when the
administration switches from one party to the other. James

Berryman was educated in the Washington public schools, Georgetown University and the Corcoran Art School, all in the District of Columbia. As a young man he put in a year on the Alberqueque, N.M., *State Tribune,* which no doubt gave him something of a national outlook, but did not alter his basic attitude, that of the old-style Federalist.

The influence of a cartoonist is not measurable by any known criterion, but the sturdy common sense of the Berrymans, father and son, has probably affected the government to an extent hardly guessed by historians.

28. Hats

Reginald W. Manning, 1951

Reginald W. Manning's "Hats," published in the Phoenix *Arizona Republic* in 1950 and awarded the Pulitzer Prize the next year, has a strong claim to be called the most characteristically American cartoon in the series, for it reflects the very strong American prejudice against both war and diplomacy, and a cartoon that reflects one of our strongest prejudices certainly has a national flavor. Incidentally, this drawing is noteworthy also for its technical excellence, for it makes its point with the absolute minimum of fuss. It is hard to see how one line could be erased without wrecking the cartoon, or how one could be added without weakening it.

At the same time a cynic can argue plausibly that the popularity of this cartoon in 1950 exposes a good deal of what is wrong with America. The simplification of the drawing is admirable, but the simplification of thought that it represents is not. The white cross in Korea carries one hat only, an American helmet. In that it is falsified. It should carry as many as the hat tree at Lake Success, for Koreans and British and Turks and Greeks and many others, as well as Americans, died in Korea, and the American helmet was relatively no more important there than the American top hat was at Lake Success.

But it was then and undoubtedly still is the choice of millions of Americans to regard Korea as an exclusively American show, while at the United Nations we are lost in the crowd. It is not an attractive characteristic. It is, in fact, evidence of discouraging political immaturity to assume that we do all the work while other people have all the fun; it is the attitude not merely of a small boy, but one of the whining type.

The Korean war did not produce as much sniveling as either the War of 1812 or the Mexican War, but a good deal more than followed the Second World War. The reason is not far to seek. Victory over the dictators came in 1945, just after a Presidential election, and three years before the next one. In such circumstances there was no political profit to be gained by portraying the United States as trapped into the war by designing men against its own will—a portrayal permitting use of the most effective of all political slogans, "Turn the rascals out!"

The foundation of our political philosophy is that the average American is a pretty decent sort. If it were not so, the whole theory of democratic self-government would collapse, for men must rise well above the level of the brute to be capable of governing themselves. But decency is the measure of the average, which implies that a considerable part of the population is below that level, some permanently, but many more cyclically. Our national history bears, in fact, a disconcerting resemblance to the clinical history of a manic-depressive. The fact that occasionally we have risen above ourselves is sufficient evidence that we are capable of sinking below.

Vast numbers of Americans including, it would seem, the field commander, never understood our purpose in fighting in Korea. Whipping the North Koreans and their Chinese allies was contributory to the aim, but it was not the aim, which was to demonstrate the solidarity and strength of the free nations. General MacArthur's proclamation that "There is no substitute for victory," is conclusive proof that he never got the idea, so his removal from command was inevitable.

Many Americans don't understand it to this day, and not understanding, have done their best to defeat the purpose of the war by demonstrating a lack of solidarity among the democracies. They are determined to believe, and do all they can to make the world believe, that Korea was not the free world's response to a challenge, but at best an American adven-

Hats

LAKE
SUCCESS

KOREA

REG·MANNING

ture, and at worst President Truman's personal exploit. They have found a substitute for victory, all right. It is to reject the fruits of the victory that the soldiers have won.

They have gone far toward success. Five years after the appearance of this cartoon the democracies were so badly split that when the Egyptian, Nasser, offered a threat to peace our best friends thought they would have to force our hand, with the result that the United States found itself lined up on the side of Communist Russia against Great Britain and France. There was no solid phalanx of seventeen nations against totalitarianism this time, and the result was the humiliation of Britain and France and the immense strengthening of the Egyptain dictator, although his armies had been soundly whipped by the Israelis. Nasser, too, found a very satisfactory substitute for victory by exploiting irresolution and dissension among his enemies.

None of this, however, made any impression on those Americans who continue to believe that there was only one helmet on the mortuary cross in Korea, for there are none so blind as those who will not see.

Yet this is one instance in which there is a reasonable doubt that the committee making the award accurately represented prevailing public opinion. In fact, it was put to the test a year later, when a tremendous effort was made to commit one of the major parties to the theory that the United States can and should pursue its own course without acknowledging any obligation to support liberty whenever and wherever it is seriously threatened. That effort was defeated when Eisenhower beat Taft in the nominating convention, and in the subsequent election won a tremendous vote of approval, even though his party lagged behind.

It would seem, then, that this cartoon actually reflected the view of a minority of a minority. Its choice can still be defended on technical grounds, but that sets it somewhat apart from the others, all of which have been studied not as examples of craftsmanship, but as mirrors reflecting the sinuosities of American thought. We did not go isolationist in 1950 or later, although it must be admitted that our course since has been decidedly wavering. Even today some hope and more fear that the isolationist view may yet prevail.

History supports that view. Maintenance of a coalition has always been the acid test of diplomacy. It is not easy even for the duration of hostilities, and after their cessation it has hitherto been impossible. The titanic coalition that subdued Hitler, Mussolini and Tojo began to split even before the death of Roosevelt, one of whose last utterances was a warning that Russia was breaking away. Probably history will remember Roosevelt's successor chiefly because he managed to hold the remaining fragments together even after he had lost the powerful assistance of Churchill.

The normal course of a coalition that has won a war is either to fall to pieces or to consolidate into an empire. Thoughtful Americans can see little but disaster in either, and they have hoped desperately that this generation may experience a mutation that will set history at naught. For seven years—greatly assisted by the Korean episode—that hope glowed, and if it has been flickering since Suez, still, as these lines are written, it has not been extinguished, not even by the Muscovite moons. Who knows? Perhaps it will still be flickering when this page comes under the reader's eye; and if so, the fact will be momentous.

DIGRESSION ON THE MAN

Reginald West Manning, born in Kansas City, Missouri, but after the age of fourteen a resident of Phoenix, Arizona, began his career as a photographer but before he was thirty had shifted into drawing, beginning on the Phoenix *Arizona Republic,* although his work was soon syndicated to many newspapers.

He is perhaps the most versatile artist in the series of prize-winners. Not only does he draw cartoons, but he is a designer of stationery, jewelry and fabrics, and the author and publisher of picture books. He is a striking demonstration of what we like to consider a characteristic American quality, a man's ability to turn his hand to almost anything that needs to be done.

However at fifty-three—he was born in 1905—the production in which Manning took most pride was neither picture, jewel nor fabric, but a son who had become a jet pilot in the United States Air Force; and few will care to deny that this pride is his most American trait.

29. Your Editors Ought to Have More Sense Than to Print What I Say!

Fred L. Packer, 1952

F red L. Packer, of the New York *Mirror,* landed the prize in 1952 with a cartoon that touched one of the sorest spots in American journalism. "Classified!" is the caption and it depicts a bureaucrat shouting at a group of newsmen, "You editors ought to have more sense than to print what I say!"

Many, perhaps most, laymen accepted this as burlesque but it is actually an understatement of the case, as became apparent in 1957, when the administration proposed legislation the effect of which would be to make reporters and editors criminally liable for the mistakes of idiots in public office. Packer's jobholder did no more than accuse the editors of having no sense; the administration would charge them with moral turpitude if they failed to retrieve the errors of official fools and rogues. It is clear then that the cartoonist understated the situation.

Toleration of secrecy in the conduct of public affairs had been increasing steadily for ten years before publication of this cartoon. In the beginning it had been a military necessity. To fight Germany and Japan without concealing not only our troop movements, but also our sources and lines of supply, would have been nothing short of insane. Press and public both realized it and submitted to censorship willingly and, with only two or three ugly exceptions, loyally.

But the secrecy necessary to military commanders is also a great comfort and convenience to civilian officeholders. In a democracy officeholders are accountable, in the last analysis, to the public. Obviously, no accounting can be made to the public in secret, so secrecy as a governmental policy has the effect of releasing officeholders from accountability. Naturally, they favor it, and none more strongly than those who are only dimly, if at all aware of their own incompetence or venality.

On the other hand, one of the most important functions of the press is to keep the public constantly informed of the way in which its business is being conducted. Secrecy makes difficult and at times impossible the discharge of this function. Naturally, journalists hate it, and this guarantees incesssant warfare between the press and the censors.

For the duration of active hostilities this warfare was suspended because military necessity overrode all other considerations; but in 1945 it flared up again, and the press found its position seriously impaired. For one thing, the American public had become psychologically conditioned to acceptance of censorship and did not support freedom of the press with its old-time vigor. For another, the cease-fire was not followed by a tranquil peace, but by an intense ideological struggle—the "cold war" with Russia and her allies—and a great deal of military thinking was carried over into this nonmilitary struggle. One idea carried over from the hot to the cold war was that of the necessity of censorship.

As far as the designing and manufacture of weapons is concerned this was logical enough. Death-dealing engines are not employed in a cold war, and their fabrication in times of technical peace is a safeguard against the possible transformation of the war from cold to hot. But it did not stop there. The policy of secrecy was applied to a vast number of things that had only the remotest connection with the work of the armorers; and in a war of nerves this is what the doctors call contra-indicated, that is to say, the very thing you ought not to do.

The supreme weapon in a cold war is not fire, but terror, and fear of the unknown is the most swiftly and completely disabling of all forms of terror. Therefore to deprive the enemy of the use of this form of terror is an objective of great importance, and it is achieved by reducing as far as possible the field of the unknown. Even in a hot war, early and accurate information rarely has as disastrous an effect upon morale as

'CLASSIFIED!'

the product of the rumor-factories; and in a cold war, that is, a war of ideas, accurate information is indispensable to success.

Nobody denies this in theory, but in practice its application is difficult to the point of impossibility unless very high authority demands its application. The reason is simple. In practice it frequently means requiring a man to broadcast the fact that he has made a fool of himself, and nobody will do that except under compulsion.

So for ten years and more the press has fought a losing battle to obtain access to full information about the conduct of public affairs. In the field of foreign relations it has been especially difficult. By 1957, when the Chinese regime offered to admit a limited number of American reporters, the State Department refused at first to countenance their going, and in the ensuing debate it was revealed that the Secretary of State regarded the press as properly an arm of the government, as definitely, if not as completely, subject to control as the Army and Navy.

Fifty years ago such a doctrine would have set off an explosion of popular wrath that would have blown the administration out of office. It did nothing of the kind in 1957. Without doubt this apathy is partially explained by a change in the public attitude toward government. Two tremendous wars, followed by a pseudo-peace, not the real thing, have accustomed us to governmental discipline which can verge on tyranny with relative immunity.

But there remains the probability that in some measure it also reflects a change in the attitude of the public toward the press. Within the past fifty years the press—that is, the periodical press, newspapers and magazines as apart from books—has become Big Business in a way that would have startled Joseph Pulitzer, to say nothing of Dana, Greeley, Freneau and Benjamin Franklin. Bureaucracy itself is no more partial to secrecy than is Big Business, and since the press has risen to that rank it has taken on many of the attributes of Big Business. So it is torn by opposing impulses—its social function is publicity, yet its economic function draws it toward secrecy, and the resultant is partial impotence in the war against the censors.

Realization by the public that it is no more possible for a poor man to own a big-city newspaper than it is for him to own a railroad leads to the inference that the American Newspaper Publishers' Association is essentially a millionaires' club, and no millionaires' club has ever been seriously considered as the palladium of the people's liberties. When the publishers make moan about the arrogant and tyrannical conduct of bureaucrats toward newspapers, the common man too often feels that even if these rich men were informed there is no guarantee that they would pass the information undiluted to the common man. Hence when freedom of the press is abridged, the indignation of the public is not too hard to keep under control.

This is probably the people's mistake. Careful examinations by persons certainly not biased in favor of the press have shown that during the Presidential compaign of 1956 deliberate slanting of the news in favor of one party was by no means universal and less widely prevalent than many had supposed. However, when Ye Editor runs with the millionaires, stones will be bounced off his ribs as inevitably as they were off Old Dog Tray's, when he ran with the sheep-killing pack.

DIGRESSION ON THE MAN

Fred Little Packer is not only a Native Son, but the place of his birth was Hollywood. That, however, was in 1886, long before Hollywood had become the tinsel capital of Never-Never Land, and Packer followed a normal course through the Los Angeles public schools, then the Los Angeles School of Art and Design, and finished off with two years at the Chicago Art Institute.

His journalistic career was somewhat intermittent. After working awhile for the *Examiner,* of his home town, and the *Call,* of San Francisco, he came East in 1919 and for twelve years gave his attention entirely to book and magazine illustration and commercial art. Not until 1932 did he resume political cartooning for the New York *Journal.* There he caught the eye of the late Arthur Brisbane, and when Brisbane was transferred to editorship of the *Mirror* he took Packer along.

Brisbane died in 1936, but by that time Packer was so thoroughly established with the *Mirror* that he needed no patron, and fifteen years later he brought the paper the distinction of the Pulitzer Prize.

30. Aftermath

Edward D. Kuekes, 1953

F ive days after the election of 1952 Edward D. Kuekes published the prize-winning cartoon of that year in the Cleveland *Plain Dealer*. In it he reflected one of the most widespread popular superstitions in America—the myth that the striated muscles and the cerebral cortex develop synchronously, which is the basic support of the fallacy that when a man is old enough to fight, he is old enough to vote. This can be sustained only on the theory that in voting a man's legs are as much a measure of his competence as his brain.

The drawing depicts a pair of soldiers carrying a casualty off the field—presumably in Korea—on a stretcher. One inquires, "Wonder if he voted?" The other replies, "No, he wasn't old enough."

The delusion that this makes a point is so widespread that it seems to be shared by the President of the United States, and in the state of Georgia it had already been made the basis of legislation reducing the minimum voting age to eighteen years. This weights the electoral scales still more heavily on the side of immaturity; and many careful observers are convinced that they are already dangerously overweighted on that side.

The theory that a man should not be called on to defend the country until he is old enough to participate in its management is based on the very old American belief in the volunteer soldier. It is a belief basically unsound in a democracy except as it relates to men who choose one of the services as a career, the officers and men of the regular establishment. They should

AFTERMATH

Reproduced by permission of Edward Kuekes and the *Cleveland Plain Dealer*

be volunteers. But as regards men who take up arms only in an emergency, the volunteer is taking to himself authority to make a decision that is not rightfully his to make.

In time of war the difference between victory and defeat may be exactly the difference between correct and incorrect disposition of the country's manpower. The assignment of manpower to the place where it will do most good is a tricky and difficult business, requiring a vast amount of information and much careful thought. No individual has the necessary information, no draft board has all it needs, and a community is lucky if the combined brains of its draft board are equal to doing, not a perfect job, but a passable one.

Our concept of the volunteer was formed back in the days when wars were limited and were fought by armies and navies. In those days it was practicable for a man to go to war or not go, according to his circumstances and inclinations. But with the beginning of total wars, fought not merely by the armed services but by whole nations, the question of going or not going was no longer a question. We all go. In the Second World War London and Berlin were among the bloodiest of the battlefields. In the next war Washington, Chicago and New York will be battlefields and among the casualties women and children will very likely outnumber soldiers.

In such a war the question, Shall I take part? is answered before it is asked. You shall take part. The only uncertainty is the location of your post of duty. In military operations it would be obviously preposterous to leave to each man the selection of his own post. When the whole population is engaged, that reasoning applies to the whole population.

In the next world war the babies in St. Louis, in the heart of the continent, will be in as great danger as the babies in Tokyo were in the last one; and the babies in Tokyo died in large numbers. Shall we say, then, that because the babies were old enough to be killed in battle, the babies should be allowed to vote?

Military authorities agree that for active service in a theater of war the requisites are, first, excellent muscular coordination, second, physical endurance and, third, intelligence enough to understand orders, even when they are somewhat complicated.

Physiologists agree that these capabilities normally are developed in the order in which they are named. The sense of hearing, for example, is said to be keener at the age of fifteen than at any earlier or later age, but muscular strength does not reach its top until some years after hearing has begun to decline. Taking all factors into consideration, the ideal recruit is a man somewhere between the ages of eighteen and twenty-seven. The quality of endurance, it is true, comes somewhat later. During the Sinai campaign of 1956 the Army of Israel found that the unit that could outmarch all the others over that very difficult terrain was a brigade of second-string reservists averaging between thirty and thirty-five years of age.

Finally, psychologists agree that the muscles and the brain practically never reach their highest point of development at the same time. The lag there is a long one. A baseball player, or a prize-fighter, is old at thirty-five, and if he leads the league in batting, or scores a knock-out at that age, all the world wonders; but a lawyer who should be named Chief Justice of the United States at thirty-five would be regarded as an infant prodigy. A lawyer doesn't win his victories with his arms and shoulders, or he would be out as soon as the athlete.

The answer to the question of when a man should begin to vote therefore depends on whether or not voting is a form of athletics, as war certainly is, or a form of cerebral activity, as the practice of law is. It is hardly to be questioned that an American election is widely regarded as a sporting event. The immense sums of money that change hands on the outcome prove it. But the spin of the ball on a roulette wheel is also a sporting event, yet not athletics; for that matter, bets have been made on the verdict that a jury would return in a court of law.

Those who contend that an election, while a contest, is not an athletic contest, have logical grounds for maintaining that if the minimum age for voting is to be changed at all, it should be moved to twenty-five, rather than to eighteen. This would afford more time for a man's thinking capacity to catch up with his fighting capacity. If the vast majority of electors thought more and fought less during a political campaign, the effect on government would certainly be appreciable and probably would be salubrious.

No important political leader has as yet come out in favor

of a voting age of twenty-five, and probably none ever will. The sentimental notion that defending the country is properly a voluntary activity leads to the inference that special privileges are due those who undertake it. But it is a *non sequitur* that participating in government should be one of such privileges. This is an effectual block; for politicians who agree on nothing else are at one in the opinion that he who does battle against sentimentality in the United States is a whipped man from the start.

Digression on the Man

Edward Daniel Kuekes was born in Pittsburgh, Pennsylvania, but his family moved to Ohio while he was still a boy, and he grew up there, was educated at Baldwin-Wallace college at Berea, at the Cleveland School of Art and the Chicago Academy of Fine Arts, so his standing as a Midwesterner is hardly impaired by the accident of birth in the East.

He had worked for the *Plain Dealer* for thirty-two years when he won the prize, beginning with commercial art and becoming chief political cartoonist in 1949. His professional faith is simple; a good cartoonist, he says, resembles a good golfer in that the fewer strokes he makes the better.

Kuekes also works in pastels and etching, but for relaxation, not for fame; and in the same spirit he raises orchids and plays the musical bells. The *Plain Dealer* is said to have carried more than two hundred of his cartoons on the front page as well as those he contributes to the editorial page—evidence not merely of his energy, but of an iron endurance, which is a necessary qualification for a man who is to last a long time at what is unquestionably a nerve-grinding occupation.

To say of any veteran cartoonist that he is a sturdy specimen is redundant; he wouldn't have lasted to be a veteran if he were not.

31. You Were Always a Great Friend of Mine, Joseph

Herbert L. Block, 1954

I n 1954 Herbert L. Block returned to the front with a cartoon on the death of Joseph Stalin, which the Washington *Post* had published right after the event in 1953. "Herblock," now developed into one of the most powerful cartoonists in America, and one of its keenest wits, in this drawing is utterly grim. Stalin, armed with a sickle dripping blood, is conducted into the blank unknown by Death, bearing a huge scythe on his shoulder. The spectre remarks, "You were always a great friend of mine, Joseph."

The words are simple but the drawing thunders like old Raleigh, three centuries ago: "O eloquent, just, and mightie Death! whom none could advise, thou hast perswaded; what none hath dared, thou hast done . . ."

In the presence of the "eloquent, just, and mightie" the sometime dictator is reduced to a little man with a little sickle, trudging into oblivion—little, and weak, and pitiful, yes, pitiful, even though the little sickle drips blood. Less than five years after his death it was already apparent that the most striking characteristic of the crimes of Stalin was their utter futility. What did it avail to stave in Trotzky's skull with a pickax? The plotting went right ahead without him, and all the Old Bolsheviki had to go, yet still the shadow of fear hung over the Kremlin. Starving two million peasants did not make the agricultural system work. Slaughtering the generals did not enable the Red army to stand up against Hitler's first insane assault. No crime produced its intended effect. All were useless, all wasted effort.

In the nature of things dictators are all friends of Death, but not all of them are as hopelessly dull as this fellow. For instance, Mussolini's clowning at times added to the gaiety of nations, especially when he postured as Julius Caesar. The cream of the jest was that he seemed to enjoy it himself. Hitler apparently had a touch of Satanic genius, and the paroxysms into which he used to work himself at Nuremberg no doubt gave him moments of ecstasy. But can anyone imagine that Stalin ever had a good time? Even drunk, he glowered rather than giggled, and sober there was no duller dog on earth.

The world has given him the benefit of the doubt in assuming that he nerved the Russians to that last desperate stand at Stalingrad, but Khrushchev has raised a doubt, even as to that. It is plain enough that distance and cold finished the Germans, as they had finished the French in 1812. But Khrushchev in his famous indictment asserted that it was only Stalin's initial blundering that permitted the Germans to reach Stalingrad at all. If, then, the credit of stiffening Russian resistance is taken from him, there is no interest in him whatever, except a morbid interest in his bloody hands.

The one close parallel with Stalin that history has to offer was Philip II, of Spain, who also was gloomy, leaden, cruel and crafty, without being intelligent. But the really shocking parallel is the way in which each threw away a brilliant opportunity. Each was the heir of a great man—Philip the legitimate heir of Charles V, who, abdicating, handed over to his son half the world; Stalin the illegitimate heir of Lenin, who, dying, could not prevent Stalin from seizing the re-instituted empire of the czars.

But they inherited more than great material possessions. When Philip came to the throne Pizzaro had been dead fifteen years and Cortez, eight. The fabulous wealth of Peru and Mexico was pouring into Spain in such quantities that it revolutionized the price structure of all Europe and created modern capitalism. But in addition to the gold and silver, Spain had been rejuvenated, morally and intellectually. During his reign Cervantes "smil'd Spain's chivalry away," Lope de

"You Were Always A Great Friend Of Mine, Joseph"

Vega turned out most of his eighteen hundred plays, Gongora was still enriching, not yet ruining Spanish poetry, and El Greco was inspiring new life in Spanish painting. Philip was monarch of a vibrant nation, magnificently equipped to lead European civilization.

Stalin succeeded to no such fabulous riches, but he also obtained control of a nation vibrantly alive. Nikolai Lenin had to an astounding degree the mysterious faculty of inspiring his followers, and in Leon Trotzky he had an organizing and administrative genius little, if any, inferior to Charles V. Between them they had liberated the minds as well as the bodies of the Russian masses, and the surge of life through that country astonished the world, dazzling the extremists of the left and scaring the wits out of extremists of the right. Even moderates began to suspect that they might live to see fulfillment of Tocqueville's prophecy that Russia would one day lead half the world to a higher civilization.

But a pair of dour fanatics frustrated the hope in both cases. Philip dissipated the resources of Spain in a series of useless and senseless wars, and crushed its intelligence under the weight of a savage bigotry. Stalin twice—in 1934 and again in 1945— churlishly struck aside the hand of friendship extended to him and confined Russia in the prison of his own dark spirit. Philip started Spain down a decline from which she has never recovered. Stalin, instead of making Russia the leader of civilization, has made it the terror of civilization by crushing its liberal energies under the weight of a bigotry worse than Philip's.

Friends of Death they both were, friends of Death dictating to life. The world has seen tyrants, and villainous ones too, who yet possessed talents that made their passing half regretted even by men who love liberty. Charles V was one. He was a friend of life at least in the sense that he brought order out of chaos. So did Napoleon. As for the crimes of that very bloody dynasty, the Medici, they have been brushed aside by the world's admiration of their love of art, the flower of life.

But no tinge of that attaches to Joseph Stalin. Herblock has drawn him with his back turned, and why not? His big nose, big mustache and big pipe made him easy to caricature, but to what end? He was a friend of Death and that's that. He apparently had no happiness himself, and he certainly gave none to anybody else, so now that he is gone, who cares, who wishes to remember what he looked like?

Herblock is not ordinarily a grim cartoonist, and this drawing is somewhat out of character for him. But there is no manner of doubt that it reflected the mood of the country in 1953, or that the mood persists to this day, to the limited extent that anybody thinks about Stalin at all.

Yet a mighty dictator he was, in his time. His failure was not any failure of power, or energy, or craft; it was simply that he cultivated the wrong friend, and that friend has served him in the fashion that Sir Walter described: "Thou hast drawne together all the farre stretched greatnesse, all the pride, crueltie, and ambition of man, and covered it all over with these two narrow words, *Hic jacet!*"

DIGRESSION ON THE MAN

Herbert Lawrence Block, not yet fifty and physically hale, needs one more win to come abreast of Kirby and Duffy, two to surpass them both, and he will probably do it.

One strong reason for this prediction is the fact that he is not only a master craftsman, but also to a large extent a free man. The credit for this goes in no small part to Eugene Meyer, a publisher too intelligent to damage a valuable property by meddling. When he put Herblock on the Washington *Post*, it was with the understanding that if the cartoonist got a little out of line with editorial policy it would not be held against him, provided the cartoon was effective.

As a result, on more than one occasion the editorial columns and the cartoon have sworn at each other; but the reading public, far from taking offense, has been disposed to laugh and cheer whenever it occurred. Such incidents merely added to the *Post*'s reputation as a really representative newspaper, not a partisan or factional organ.

Block is rated as a liberal, although not with his consent. He will neither confirm nor deny the report on the ground that he doesn't know what a liberal is. But one thing is certain —he will never be received with enthusiasm in any congregation of Stuffed Shirts, which is distinction indeed.

32. How Would Another Mistake Help?

Daniel R. Fitzpatrick, 1955

Daniel R. Fitzpatrick won again in 1955 with a cartoon that is incomprehensible without some attention to the time and the place. The place of publication was St. Louis, the medium the *Post-Dispatch*, and the time a moment when a vociferous, if not very numerous party in this country demanded interference by the United States in Indo-China, where the French were losing a war against native Communists, supported by Red China.

The United States had no important interest in Indo-China other than its general interest in preventing the spread of Communism. But that general interest, plus the topography of this country, had divided our people, and St. Louis, on the Mississippi River, was close to the line of division. It is often regarded as bad form to admit that Americans are divided, but it is bad judgment to ignore the fact.

The United States, like most continental areas, consists of what Toynbee calls the Desert and the Sown. Of course the terms are not absolute. The Desert is inhabited, and the Sown is not completely cultivated; but where agriculture is capable of supporting a large population is the Sown; where it is not is the Desert.

In this country the Sown is divided into unequal parts by what used to be called, until real-estate agents made it scandalous to use the term, the Great American Desert, the relatively waterless area lying between meridians 100 and 115

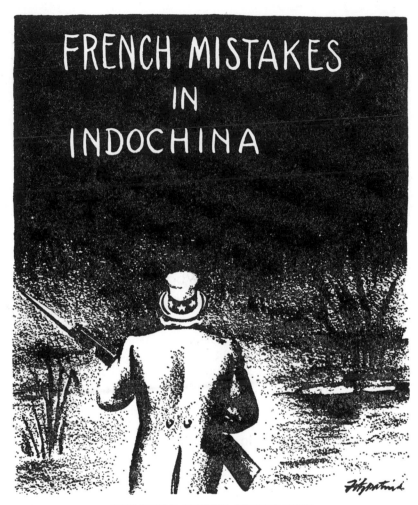

FRENCH MISTAKES IN INDOCHINA

HOW WOULD ANOTHER MISTAKE HELP?

west—on the Mexican border about a thousand, on the Canadian about seven hundred miles wide. West of the Desert lies the strip of five hundred miles of the Sown comprising the Pacific slope; east of it fifteen hundred miles of Sown, comprising the Mississippi Valley and the Atlantic slope.

When war exploded on both sides of us in 1941 each of these divisions of the Sown devoted most of its attention to the war nearest at hand. Washington's decision was that the heart of enemy strength was the Nazi-Fascist Axis, which should be destroyed first, with Japan merely held in check to be attended to later. The Pacific slope never forgave this decision, even though the event justified it, for the smaller forces assigned to the holding operation—essentially naval warfare—not only checked Japan, but had her virtually defeated by the time the Axis was reduced. We had barely begun transferring Eisenhower's army to MacArthur's command when the enemy, hit twice by the atomic bomb, capitulated.

Then when it became plain that the war had not really ceased, but had only turned cold, the same division reappeared. It seemed to Washington that Red Russia constituted the dangerous threat, but to the extreme West it was Red China, and Washington's preoccupation with Russia became as irritating as was its former preoccupation with the Berlin-Rome Axis. The Korean affair strengthened the West's belief, which spread across the Desert even as far as St. Louis. It was felt by Fitzpatrick and his cartoon is aimed at it. It is actually an effort at communication between Americans.

The occasion was the western response to the collapse of French colonial power in Indo-China. A French army of 16,000 men lacking a competent intelligence service had moved into a trap at Dienbienphu and was lost. But the basic failure lay far behind this military fiasco. It was the inability of the French, during an occupation of more than fifty years, to win the loyal support of the natives even to the extent that we had won the loyalty of the Filipinos in forty years. Indo-China saw nothing comparable to the Battle of the Bataan Peninsula, where Filipinos and Americans died side by side.

Nevertheless many westerners, fearing the extension of Red China's power, demanded that the United States intervene as it had intervened in Korea, and even the Secretary of State seemed momentarily inclined to that view. But the situations were entirely different. In the first place, the South Koreans were not colonials, but independent people fighting for their own land. In the second place, the United States did not act on its own, but on the authority of the United Nations, and no such mandate could be obtained for an intervention in Indo-China; yet without it intervention would have been unmistakably an imperialist war.

This is the view that Fitzpatrick took in his cartoon, and it was unquestionably the view of the majority. But it was not then, is not now, and perhaps never will be the view of the Pacific slope. That slope looks to the Orient, the Atlantic slope to the occident, and the difference in outlook must always affect American foreign policy. There is a divergence of interest among the sections, and it may not disappear but rather be accentuated as population increases and competition for the means of subsistence sharpens. We deceive ourselves when we attempt to deny it; the only sensible course is to adjust our thinking to fit the fact.

Three years after this cartoon was published another failure of communication between the sections became glaringly apparent in the matter of racial segregation in the schools. Neither North nor South was prepared for the iron determination exhibited by the other, or much disposed to heed Jefferson's warning: "While the will of the majority is in all cases to prevail, that will, to be rightful, must be reasonable." There was no real meeting of minds on the point of what is reasonable, and a definite weakening of the nation is the result.

The blackest grief of a forest ranger's life is the fact that while you are beating out the flames in front, the woods take fire behind you; and a statesman's life is much the same. Every careful student of international relations knows that the gravest obstacle in the way of permanent peace is the difficulty, often the complete breakdown of communication between peoples. Most Americans believe that if the Russian people understood what the American people really want, the cold war would evaporate overnight. Which raises suspicion that if *we* understood what *they* really want, the same result might be achieved.

So much is plain to the dullest and justifies the most energetic effort to remove the barrier of misunderstanding among the nations. But in the midst of the struggle we cannot afford to overlook the possibility that the woods may take fire behind us—that we may permit sectional misconceptions within our borders to smoulder and creep until some gust of passion causes them to flare up in a blaze that will impede and perhaps defeat our best efforts in the international field.

"The heathen Chinee is peculiar"—it is a fact that cannot be denied. But so is the heathen Mississippian to the Michigander, and the Damyankee to the Unreconstructed Rebel. How incredible these Americans are!

Digression on the Man

Fitzpatrick, a double winner, long ago attained a position in the Middle West comparable to that of Darling, as not so much a craftsman as an institution. For one thing, he is a marvel of industry; it is said that in forty-five years he turned out fourteen thousand cartoons for the St. Louis *Post-Dispatch*.

But he was much more than prolific. He understood his people. He had a sharp eye for their quirks and perversities, but he also knew their strength and had a marvelous facility at appealing to it.

This is, of course, the test that determines a man's eligibility to be listed among the masters of the craft. The appeal to prejudice and obscurantism is easy, but an effective appeal to enlightenment is one of the most difficult things in the world. Merely to appeal is easy enough for any intelligent man, but to make an effective appeal strains the seams of the most capable. The trap is the dreadful ease with which virtue can be made odious by the slightest touch of pomposity.

Fitzpatrick did it infallibly for more than a generation; and this lifted him from the level of a mere journalist to that of a social force. The announcement in June 1958 that he would retire on the first of August signalized the close of a wonderful career.

33. Achilles

Robert York, 1956

Greatly daring, Robert York of the Louisville, Kentucky, *Times,* employed a classical allusion in the caption of a cartoon published September 16, 1955. He was daring because a classical allusion is regarded as deadly today. But York was awarded the Pulitzer Prize in 1956, although it may be doubted that half the readers of the *Times* got the point, for who tells the story of Achilles to modern schoolboys?

A generation ago it would have been safe enough, for then practically everybody who could read had been told that the sea goddess, Thetis, wishing to make her new-born son invulnerable, dipped the baby in the magic water of the river Styx, by which he was rendered immune in every part except the heel by which his mother held him. Many years later skulking Paris shot him in the heel with an arrow, thereby ending the career of the greatest of the heroes and giving to literature the phrase "Achilles' heel" as a metaphor for a vulnerable spot.

But if York's caption goes back to ancient Greece, his drawing comes right down to the minute. Obese Prosperity, given neither heart nor head, but with an immense belly, is draped like the traditional ambassador in frock coat and striped trousers, his waistcoat crossed by a ponderous watch-chain. But the one shoe that is visible is a ruin; his toes stick out in front, and behind is a large hole labeled "Farm Prices," the exposed heel of Achilles. The humor of the thing is the utter defeat of pomposity—always the triumph of satire.

York's immediate target is, of course, the silly prater who claims that all is well with the economy when the primary producers are in distress, the kind of reassurance that Coolidge and Mellon gave the country in 1928, when we were heading straight into the crash of 1929. But the cartoon goes beyond that; it exposes a fallacy that is not confined to politicians by any means, but permeates all strata of society.

This is the fallacy that free private enterprise can operate in a controlled market.

Naturally, we do not put it to ourselves so baldly. Free private enterprise in a controlled market is a contradiction in terms. If the market is controlled, enterprise is not free; so we elude the dilemma by denying that the market is controlled. Unfortunately, denying a fact does not remove it; it only confuses thinking and prevents an intelligent solution of problems.

Wherever tariffs, subsidies and monopolies exist the market is to some extent controlled. They all exist in this country and have existed for a very long time. They are so strongly rooted in the American economic system that to tear them out suddenly would certainly do more harm than good. But to maintain them and then deny that we maintain them is to introduce an element of fraud into the system; and a fraudulent economy inevitably produces evil results.

The American farmer, the primary producer, sells in a free and buys in a controlled market. Therefore the farmer is wide open to exploitation that in the past has not stopped short of outright robbery. This is a fact, and no denials will change it.

Highly productive agriculture is the mudsill of a sound economy. It is only the foundation, but all the other parts of the structure rest upon that foundation. This also is a fact.

But not until the second quarter of the twentieth century did we face these facts and begin to draw the inescapable inference, namely, that the first objective of our economic policy should be to keep agriculture operating on a high level of efficiency; and when we did begin to draw the inference we perpetrated one blunder after another, and are still blundering.

So York observes us walking abroad, presumably in a top hat, certainly in frock coat and striped trousers—and with our toes sticking out of our shoes!

ACHILLES

Reproduced by permission of Robert York and the *Louisville* (Ky.) *Times*

Our initial mistake, after we had at last come to the point of doing something, was to assume that since the farmer must buy in a controlled market, he ought to sell in the same kind of market. Accordingly we have made elaborate and increasingly frantic efforts to control the seller's market by reducing agricultural production. To reduce agricultural production obviously weakens the foundation of the whole economy, but that is a risk that we felt we had to take.

The outcome has been a series of measures increasingly expensive and consistently ineffective. Our farm policy has been so completely divorced from reality that the voters are now ready to believe anything that may be told about it. Perhaps Secretary of Agriculture Wallace did not advocate plowing under the pigs, nor Secretary Benson, plowing under the farmers, but most of the country thinks they did.

One man did indeed come up with a highly original idea, to wit, that what our Achilles should do is get a new pair of shoes, but that was hooted down as completely insane. This man was Charles F. Brannan, who suggested that the farmer should not be forced to sell in any market, free or controlled, but should be paid for producing, letting others handle the product after he had brought it to the market.

The consensus among politicians seemed to be that, as the Brannan Plan seemed to make sense, and as it is well known that no farm policy makes sense, therefore the Brannan Plan could not be a real farm policy, and it was promptly heaved overboard. It is true that some years later Secretary Benson salvaged a bit of it and applied it in the case of wool; but it is still an article of faith among the political pundits that anyone who adheres to the Brannan Plan is touched in the head and cannot possibly be taken seriously.

But since we cannot let the farmers starve on pain of starving ourselves, we guarantee him ninety, or eighty-two and a half, or seventy-five per cent of parity—parity being a price that would put him on a level with other producers—and he produces terrifically. Whereupon the government must buy a large part of the product. But we lock up the stuff, or try to dump it abroad, or do anything with it except sell it at low prices to industrial workers in the cities. For that might bring down the cost of living, and that, in turn, might disturb the general price structure, and to disturb the price structure is the political Unpardonable Sin.

A patch here, and a patch there, a half-sole, a heel-tap, a replaced tongue—but never, under any circumstances, a new pair of shoes—such has been our farm policy for thirty-five years. When the problem first became acute in 1932 milk farmers in the Middle West had to be squelched by troops, because they were halting trucks and pouring the milk into roadside ditches. So by 1957 we had made such progress that milk farmers in the Middle West were halting trucks and pouring the milk in roadside ditches.

Like Father Divine's peace—prosperity, it's wonderful! Our Achilles is resplendent from the top of his hat to the bottom of his trousers. But he still walks with a limp, and there is still danger that at any moment he may stub an exposed toe and fall on his face.

Digression on the Man

Robert York, born in Minneapolis in 1909, lived in Des Moines for a while and received instruction there from Jay N. Darling. But what he got from Ding was certainly not technique, for the styles of the two men are completely different. It is a fact, though, that the sardonic humor in York's work is strongly reminiscent of the older man's.

York got his technical proficiency at the Chicago Academy of Fine Arts, and worked for a while on the *Tribune,* of that city, but not as a cartoonist. His first job in that line was with the Nashville, Tennessee, *Banner,* but twenty years ago he went to the *Times,* of Louisville, and was there when he won the prize with a cartoon that he thought would never be considered in an election year.

Politically, he admits to being "a bit on the liberal side," although a good many observers would alter that to the realistic side. Come to think of it, though, is there a difference? The Egghead has his fantasies, but that they are any more extravagant than those of the Squarehead is certainly open to doubt.

34. Wonder Why My Parents Didn't Give Me Salk Shots

Tom Little, 1957

T om Little, of the Nashville *Tennessean,* was the man in 1957, winning with a cartoon that is social, not political satire. It was drawn to support the campaign in 1956 for the widest possible use of the Salk vaccine against infantile paralysis, and portrays a small cripple wondering why his parents failed to give him the vaccine.

This is a newspaper man's cartoon in the sense that the journalist understands its force better than any other group of the population, school teachers perhaps excepted. Its target is the amazing impermeability of the human mind.

By 1956 it was established beyond reasonable doubt that the Salk vaccine does furnish an important degree of protection against poliomyelitis, and there was no indication that its administration was attended by any great risk. Furthermore, a very elaborate effort, supported by the medical profession, by state and national public health services, and by vigorous private organizations, had been made to render the vaccine available at low cost, or none at all, to every child endangered by the plague.

That is to say, there was a very strong reason for giving this protection to every child in the country. There was no strong reason, scientific or economic, for not giving it. The thing had been publicized to the very limit. Millions had been spent on all known forms of advertising, and the paid publicity was hardly a drop in the bucket by comparison with the colossal

WONDER WHY MY PARENTS DIDN'T GIVE ME SALK SHOTS?

program of free publicity. The daily press, the weekly press, the monthly press, the religious press, trade organs, fraternal organs, house organs, down to the very theater programs, had donated literally acres of space to the project, with radio and television joining their voices. Nor was the bulk of the material prepared by professional copy-writers or magazine hacks. The most eminent and respected men in the country, not doctors only, but clergymen, educators, lawyers and business men of the highest types had urged the matter upon the attention of parents and guardians. Yet in 1956 there remained millions of children who had not been protected.

To the strict logician this may be amazing, but not to newspaper men except, perhaps, cub reporters. To every experienced journalist it was a perfectly normal situation, regrettable, doubtless, but entirely usual. Newspaper men know that it is not the statement of a fact, but the ninety-ninth repetition of the statement that at last gets across to fifty-one per cent of the readers. The most powerful piece demonstrating that the man-eating shark is a hideous monster may, with luck, reach four per cent of your circulation; but when you are preparing the one hundredth editorial on the subject some character will inquire, in all innocence, "Is it true, as I hear, that your paper is opposed to the man-eating shark?" Which accounts to a considerable extent for the prevalence of stomach ulcers in the craft.

Well, they say that in 1810, within fifty miles of Paris, they discovered a peasant who had never heard of Napoleon.

So what? So, an impatient man should never go into newspaper work, or into anything else in which success depends upon persuading large numbers of people to adopt a specific point of view. Yet history does not sustain the inference that great journalists are conspicuously patient men—rather the contrary. That explains why so many of the very greatest were obviously frustrated men.

Still, the percentage of craftsmen in this work who end as mental cases is not conspicuously larger than in other lines of human endeavor. The reason is the apperception, coming slowly but surely to those who survive the first few years, that this inertia of the mass has values, as well as banes, and it is a question which predominates.

The fact that the public, taken *en masse*, is iron-skulled means that many excellent ideas are woefully slow to penetrate; but it also means that innumerable idiocies bounce off. When one stops to consider that of the total number of new ideas propounded every day those that are idiotic vastly outnumber those that are sound, the impermeability of the human mind may be not its fatal defect, but its saving grace.

"Where reason is left free to combat it," said Jefferson, error of opinion may be tolerated with safety. All of us tend to forget that essential condition of tolerance; and none forget it more quickly than honest enthusiasts who perceive the merit of a new idea so clearly that they are persuaded that the salvation of the country depends upon its immediate acceptance, and who will not wait to investigate the possible demerits that may lurk in its shadows. Adlai E. Stevenson put it neatly during his first campaign. "We all know the general," said he, referring to Eisenhower, "but who are these one-eyed guys with knives in their teeth that are climbing aboard behind him?" Stevenson spoke of individuals, but his words apply quite as aptly to ideas.

Little, in drawing this cartoon, saw the tragedy that attends the lethargy of the human mind, and for his single purpose that was all that counted. He would have broken the force of his picture had he undertaken anything else. In the matter of the Salk vaccine, indeed, the thing had been so thoroughly debated that further delay would seem to be sheer unreason, not the necessary time for reason to operate. In any event, an advocate, as the cartoonist was in this instance, is under a moral obligation to state his own case just as strongly as he can put it, leaving the statement of the other side to some opposing advocate.

In emphasizing this phase of the problem he was also reflecting the mood of a great majority of the thinking people of the country. They were genuinely and deeply disturbed by the relative slowness with which the project seemed to be moving. This makes the cartoon a marker tracing the course of social history, the record of a mood that unquestionably existed in 1956. To that extent its authenticity is beyond debate.

It is the bitterness of the thing that is open to question—not the bitterness of the individual tragedy, which cannot be overstated, but the bitterness of its social implications. If it were accepted at face value, if one could believe that stony-hearted indifference were the answer to the child's question, then one must despair of the future of the American people as a nation incapable of self-preservation, to say nothing of self-government.

But the answer is not indifference, it is inertia, and the unreserved condemnation of inertia is the aspect of the cartoon that calls for an intelligent skepticism. Mental inertia is, as a rule, deplorable, but the intelligent skeptic, distrustful of general rules, doubts that it is always and altogether deplorable. The mercurial temperament also has its drawbacks. The dull invite trouble, but not every kind of trouble. At least they escape the embarrassment, all too familiar, of those smart people who end by outsmarting themselves.

DIGRESSION ON THE MAN

Tom Little's career is exceptional in that he not only began as a writer but climbed into the executive class before he turned to cartooning. Born in Franklin, Tennessee, in 1898, he became a reporter on the *Tennessean* at the age of eighteen and a dozen years later was city editor.

But his grandfather—he was orphaned at the age of two, and grew up in his maternal grandfather's home—had taught him to draw before he could write, and the urge to use the line instead of the word eventually caught up with him, so the city editor deserted the desk for the drawing board.

It was clearly a wise move from his own standpoint as well as that of the paper, for he could get the flavor of Tennessee into a picture far better than most of his writers could get it into words. And when he added to that national distinction in the form of the Pulitzer Prize the publishers no doubt felt that even the loss of a good city editor was more than compensated.

35. The Thinker

Bruce Shanks, 1958

The winner in 1958, Bruce M. Shanks, of the Buffalo *Evening News,* reverted to what is probably the hardest-worked symbol—the figure of Uncle Sam alone excepted—in the tradition of American cartooning. This is Rodin's "The Thinker," conventionally used to represent any man, party, or institution in any kind of dilemma. In this cartoon—published September 11, 1957—The Thinker is the rank and file of organized labor, considering revelations currently being made to a Congressional investigating body usually called, from the name of its chairman, the McClellan Committee,

John L. McClellan, a Senator from Arkansas and a merciless prosecutor when he chose to be, had been having a field day. His committee was charged with the duty of looking into unethical business practices—a decorous term applying to any kind of stink—on the side of either labor or management. McClellan, a wily politician, was well aware that the term "Southern Senator" is widely regarded as a synonym for "enemy of organized labor," so he was careful to drag out a few skeletons from the management closet, giving them brief inspection and his committee an answer to charges of bias against labor; but then he began to operate on the unions, and there he really did a job.

The flat truth is that Big Labor had it coming. For the previous twenty-five years the larger unions had been rapidly accumulating wealth and power. By 1957 their treasuries were bulging and their political influence was formidable. Events had then taken the old, familiar course—"where the carcass is, there the vultures are gathered together." Along with its millions Big Labor had acquired a crew of land pirates as conscienceless as Captain Kidd's or Blackbeard's. Worming their way into high office in half a dozen big unions, they had proceeded to loot everything in sight, perhaps their nastiest bit of work being a scheme whereby a crooked labor leader and a crooked employer would get together to skin the workers and divide the swag.

All this McClellan brought to public attention with the soft delicacy of ten brass bands and a steam calliope. The uproar was such that in many minds the words "labor leader" became a term hardly less opprobrious than "pickpocket," conveying, in fact, pretty much the same impression. It was true enough that the banditti constituted only a small percentage of the country's labor leaders, but how they stank! In some measure the redolence clung to the garments of everyone in the unions, guilty or not, and as far as public confidence is concerned organized labor was set back twenty years.

It came, too, at a moment when there were alarming indications that the latest boom might be headed for the newest bust. Volume of business was declining and unemployment was increasing, which meant that the position of organized labor was already precarious. Frantic efforts were made by responsible and respectable leaders to repair the damage. The vast teamsters' union and several smaller ones were heaved bodily out of the AFL-CIO, while sanitary squads were put to work on others. This saved the movement from complete discredit, but it was heavily jarred.

So Shanks' mechanic, sitting with his chin on his fist, faces the old, bitter truth that every endeavor to improve the condition of human life has less to fear from Pontius Pilate than from Judas Iscariot.

Two things about the cartoon are worthy of special note. In the first place, it is not a reckless attack on labor. The Thinker is a victim, not a villain. So much, at least, labor has won since the days when every union was a conspiracy in the eyes of the law.

The second thing is the legend on one of the scraps of paper at his feet. It is "Fifth Amendment Dodge." This is interest-

THE THINKER

ing because it links the Fifth Amendment with the other legend, which reads, "Crooked Labor Leaders." But in these cases resort to the Fifth Amendment was no dodge, it was a legitimate reservation of defense. The question put by the McClellan Committee was not, "Did you hold certain opinions?" but "Did you steal certain moneys?"

When a man is accused of crime he has a right to trial by jury and it is perfectly correct for him to refuse to answer questions on that subject anywhere except in a court of law. Indeed, he ought to refuse, if only in defense of the principle that no man shall be held to answer for crime by any other authority than that of the courts established for the purpose.

Long, painful experience has proved that the administration of exact and equal justice is difficult under the best conditions and flatly impossible without scrupulous observance of the rules of evidence. But although experience has proved it, few of us are able to believe it at all times and with respect to all persons. We know that law and justice are not synonymous, and there have been occasions on which justice was done without law. But for every such instance there have been ninety-nine in which lawlessness wrought injustice.

In moments of calm we know it, and in a moment of calm we adopted the Fifth Amendment to protect the unpopular, although some of the unpopular are also guilty. The Fifth Amendment is an admission of our fallibility. With it, we have deliberately handcuffed ourselves in order that we may be restrained from working injustice in moments of wrath; but in moments of wrath—or of terror, or any other strong emotion— we bitterly resent the handcuffs and seek to tear them off.

Shanks' cartoon is an admission, perhaps inadvertent, that we were going through such a moment in 1957. The Fifth Amendment prevented the instant punishment of men who seemed to be arrant rogues. With regard to some of them, the estimate was not wrong. By due process of law it was proved that they were in fact arrant rogues. But the fact that the Fifth Amendment gave them temporary immunity is no reasonable basis for resenting the amendment.

Nevertheless, the popularity of this cartoon is evidence that in 1957 we did resent it—not that the cartoon was needed to establish what was common knowledge. The association of the

Fifth Amendment with crooks is a dodge all right, although not of the crooks. It is a dodge to avoid admitting that you and I need, or ever could need restraint from committing injustice. But when we refuse to admit it we are refusing to face reality, which is to say we are not in one of our great moments—not such a moment as 1791, when by adopting that amendment we proclaimed our considered opinion that it is better for some guilty to enjoy immunity than that any innocent should suffer injustice merely because they are unpopular.

That is to concede that we, the people, meaning you and me, are capable of acting wickedly toward those whom we dislike. It is humiliating, but it is true; and a great nation is one capable of accepting the truth, even at the price of humiliation. We touched the level of greatness in 1791. We have touched it since, not once but repeatedly. Yet the assumption that we have remained there always, or even for any long period is a mendacity that not Hitler with his theory of the Big Lie ever equalled.

Nevertheless, the fact that we have repeatedly been great in the past affords a reasonable presumption that we can be great in the future. It is a trying experience to live through a period in which we sink below the level of 1791 and attempt to tear down the barriers that the wise men of old erected against our own blind passion; but to mistake every such recession for a complete collapse is another departure from reality.

Big Labor got it on the point of the jaw in 1957, and Big Labor had it coming, so it was no utter calamity. But when the most belauded cartoon of the year, in commenting on the occurrence, gives a pejorative sense to invocation of the Fifth Amendment, it is not Shanks' workman alone who should prop his chin on his fist and go into profound cogitation on the state of the nation.

You and I should do some thinking, too.

Digression on the Man

Bruce M. Shanks is a home-town boy who made good right on the spot. During the war of 1941-5 he was in the Army intelligence service, but except for that interval he has spent his working life in his native city of Buffalo.

Although a first-time winner in the Pulitzer Prize list he is a cartoonist of long experience, having made his start with the Buffalo *Express* in the singular conjunction of copy boy and cartoonist. Later he worked for the *Times,* of the same city, and finally transferred to the *Evening News* in 1933. For the past quarter of a century he has been on the staff and for the past seven years editorial page cartoonist.

But although he has always lived in Buffalo he had outside recognition long before he won the Pulitzer Prize. Freedom Foundation, for instance, has laureled his work no less than four times.

Shanks' partiality for careful detail gives him the stamp of an illustrator, as well as a cartoonist. His typical cartoon is a picture, as well as an argument; and the fact that he does not lose the punch in the decoration testifies to his vigor as well as his technical skill.

The Thirty-Five

These were the prize-winning cartoons from 1922 to 1958. Taken individually, it cannot fairly be denied that each meets the stated requirement of "a distinguished example of a cartoonist's work." But if the series, taken as a whole, is a distinguished example of the American political cartoon in the thirty-seven years covered—allowing for two years in which no award was made—the inescapable inference is that the cartoon had little significant bearing upon the life of the times.

People who lived through them are convinced that these were tremendous years in the history of this country and of the world; but this is not a tremendous series. It has merit, to be sure. The mellow American humor pervades it, and it is punctuated occasionally by biting wit. There is great moral earnestness in it, and its idealistic tone can hardly be missed by the most careless observer. All of which is praiseworthy; but if American life in those years was composed entirely, or mainly of humor, wit, morality and idealism then we who survived can have little faith in our own sanity, for not many of us were fortunate enough to see it that way.

These components were included, without doubt, but theirs is not the mark set upon the period. Fury, terror, hatred and agony seared their brand upon it far more conspicuously than the gentler emotions. It can be plausibly argued that for long-continued, unremitting stress, intellectual, moral and physical, these years have no parallel in the history of the republic. Long before 1922 we had shown ourselves capable of terrific bursts of energy. The statecraft of the Constitutional Convention of 1787 was brilliant beyond all precedent—proof of an intellectual vigor unique in our annals. The political philosophy of Woodrow Wilson attained a moral elevation that idealists consider the highest we ever reached as a people. The physical energy developed in the Revolution and, above all, in the Civil War, as measured against our available resources, probably surpassed that of any later struggle. But none of these lasted thirty-seven years.

A great political cartoon is a trenchant comment on the contemporary situation, and if the situation is ugly, the cartoon should not be filled with sweetness and light. Among the things that have agitated this country since 1922 were the rise and fall of the Ku Klux Klan, the Teapot Dome scandals, the execution of Sacco and Vanzetti, the dominance and final ruin of Prohibition, the Fundamentalist revolt against intelligence culminating in the Scopes trial at Dayton, Tennessee, the panic of 1929, the Depression and the New Deal, two hot wars and a cold one. Yet the prize-winning cartoons ignore most of these things and do no more than glance at the inner significance of the rest.

To judge by the thirty-five winners one might think that the cartoonists were unaware of the most sensational events of their time, or afraid to tackle them. This is a libel on the craft. The cartoonists did see what was going on around them, and they did comment, as a rule furiously, sometimes bitterly, occasionally brutally.

Consider, for example, the most amazing phenomenon in the history of the Presidency, the career of Franklin D. Roosevelt. For nearly thirteen years the man was pictorially attacked and defended on an average of at least once a day. Allowing for leap years there are 4,748 days in thirteen years, and no extended research would be required to assemble five thousand cartoons on Roosevelt. But in this series he appears just once.

The sign manual of Rollin Kirby, the mark that made him the authority of his day, was his figure of Prohibition—a cadaverous object in a stove-pipe hat, black coat, black gloves, and large, white bow-tie, a distillation of hypocrisy. It was so effective that it was adopted by half the other cartoonists and became as conventional as the figure of Uncle Sam. But although Kirby won the Pulitzer Prize three times, this master-piece was never laureled. It was too controversial. So with Duffy's Ku Klux Klansman and Herblock's Senator McCarthy.

The rough stuff is left out. In this series Duffy's Hitler, Herblock's Stalin, Batchelor's doomed youth are figures that evoke a gasp, but there is very little else to "fright the ladies." It is beyond belief that the most chivalrous Duke would order anyone hanged for this performance, for in general the cartoonists roar as gently as any sucking dove.

It is hard to believe that this is what Joseph the Magnificent meant to encourage. Old Joe was rough stuff himself. Not only did he fight his way up every step of the way, but he did not stop fighting when he had reached the top. Pulitzer had been a millionaire for many years and was living for the most part on his yacht when his newspaper called President Theodore Roosevelt a liar, and for a long time Joe dared not land at any American port for fear of being flung into a Federal jail.

Pulitzer had no faith in the newspaper, including the newspaper cartoon, as a tranquilizer. Far from deploring controversy, he deplored the lack of it. He was aware, of course, that emotion is a treacherous guide, but he set great store by it as a spur, and in certain circumstances—as when wrong is armed and insolent—he regarded wrath as more valuable than love.

He may have been wrong. Being a fallible mortal, no doubt he was wrong in part. But he is not proved wrong by the history of the past thirty-seven years. The United States is obviously richer, more populous, and more powerful in 1958 than it was in 1922. There are some among us who are defiant enough of the cynics to hold that it is also greater. Certainly it is still a long, long way from perfection. The American citizen, as a political animal, is still the victim of his own prejudice, ignorance, and folly and probably will continue to victimize himself for many a year.

But at that he is more competent, politically, than he was in 1922. At that time he could not grasp the logic even of membership in the World Court, to say nothing of the League of Nations; while such concepts as those embodied in the Marshall Plan, and economic aid to backward nations, were miles beyond his comprehension. In domestic affairs he was not able to understand ideas as simple as collective bargaining, public policing of the markets, and equality of opportunity supported by law.

What effected the change? Not living in silks in an atmosphere laden with perfumes and soft music, one may be sure. We learned through the rough stuff. Want and fear are hideous spectres, but highly efficient pedagogues. The stinking swamps of Gaudalcanal and the Bulge, slippery with blood, argued in favor of collective security more eloquently than Woodrow Wilson ever could. The bank holiday of 1933 persuaded us that, as war should not be left to the generals, so finance is too important to be left to the bankers.

The American people came through all this by dint of courage, first of all, but powerfully aided by wrath and fear; and they came out stronger than they were at the beginning. So deprecation of the rough stuff, pushing it into the background as something that may have to be acknowledged but that is never to be emphasized, is a distortion of history.

The newspaper cartoonists have not been unmindful of this. They saw it during all these years, and they recorded it in lines that were sometimes ugly, but no uglier than truth, sometimes bitter, but no more bitter than the cup that harsh destiny pressed to the lips of the American people, and that they drained to the dregs. Many of the men represented in this volume had a distinguished part in the work; it is gratifying that they have been singled out for public honor, but the selections from their work that won the accolade are not too happy. It is rather like that letter of the Medici to the Duke of Milan commending Leonardo da Vinci as "the best lute-player in Florence."